The Formative Power of Your Congregation

The Formative Power of Your Congregation

Faith and Human Development

Christina Jones Davis and Tim Shapiro

AN ALBAN BOOK
ROWMAN & LITTLEFIELD
Lanham • Boulder • New York • London

Published by Rowman & Littlefield
An imprint of The Rowman & Littlefield Publishing Group, Inc.
4501 Forbes Boulevard, Suite 200, Lanham, Maryland 20706
www.rowman.com

86-90 Paul Street, London EC2A 4NE

Copyright © 2024 by The Rowman & Littlefield Publishing Group, Inc.

Scripture quotations are from New Revised Standard Version Bible, copyright © 1989 National Council of the Churches of Christ in the United States of America. Used by permission. All rights reserved worldwide.

All rights reserved. No part of this book may be reproduced in any form or by any electronic or mechanical means, including information storage and retrieval systems, without written permission from the publisher, except by a reviewer who may quote passages in a review.

British Library Cataloguing in Publication Information Available

Library of Congress Cataloging-in-Publication Data Available

ISBN 978-1-5381-8625-1 (cloth)
ISBN 978-1-5381-8626-8 (pbk)
ISBN 978-1-5381-8627-5 (ebook)

Contents

Acknowledgments vii

Introduction 1

PART I: CONCEPTUAL UNDERSTANDINGS AND THE CURRICULUM FRAMEWORK 15

Chapter 1: A Contextual Theology of Congregational Life 17

Chapter 2: Life Arenas 31

Chapter 3: Congregational Practices 51

Chapter 4: Trail Markers: How We Know When We Grow 67

PART II: STORIES OF FORMATION 79

Chapter 5: Forming People of Racial Reconciliation 81

Chapter 6: Forming People of Connection 101

Chapter 7: Forming a Creative Congregation 127

Chapter 8: Formative Power Imagined: A Case Study and Project Guide 141

Chapter 9: Transforming Individuals, Transforming Communities 159

Bibliography	167
Index	177
About the Authors	189

Acknowledgments

We, Christina Jones Davis and Tim Shapiro, offer this book to you because of a great cloud of witnesses who walked with us along the way. The path involved our experiences as participants in congregational life, leading classes that were part of the formative project that led to the material we offer in this book about the formative power of congregations.

We offer heartfelt thanks to the congregations that are explicitly described in the book, including New Era Church, Common Ground Church, Main Street United Methodist Church, and Witherspoon Presbyterian Church. We truly learned more from these congregations than they did from us.

Forty-five Indiana congregations participated in the *Formative Power of Your Congregation* project. Some congregations were small, some large. The community of congregations involved Black churches, Spanish-speaking churches, rural churches, multicultural churches, white churches, and more. Each church was special and unique, beautiful in remarkable ways.

We tell stories of particular congregations with their permission. We thank these congregations for trusting us to tell about their lives, religious claims, and commitments. Other illustrations in this book are composite representations, meaning they have been created by combining multiple elements, stories, and ideas to convey a concept that is true to the formative process. These composite illustrations are intended to enhance the overall understanding of the content.

I (Christina) give thanks for the ways the congregations of my youth formed me and continue to lend me support for who I am today.

Mount Zion CME Church in Ben Wheeler, Texas, located on land adjacent to the land on which my grandparents Noble and Lorene Jones, great-grandparents Nelson and Willie Jones, and great-great-grandparents Preston and Julie Hill built their homes. These grounds held much formative power for me and a long lineage of ancestors. I also want to thank Liberty Baptist Church in Atlanta, Georgia where my call to ministry was affirmed and nurtured by the late Pastor J. Sherman Pelt and the entire congregation. I want to thank the two greatest pillars of my formation, my parents the late Rev. Larry D. Jones and Virginia A. Jones, for the ways they provided intentional and loving continuity between the formation that was experienced in the church Friendship Community Bible Church in Houston, Texas where my father and Terrance S. Woodson were pastors, and that which was experienced within our home. We learned who we were as people, and whose we were, as children of God, at a young age. I am convinced that I am because these ancestral roots are.

I want to thank my current site of formation, Christian Theological Seminary, a place whose mission includes participation in God's transforming of persons and the world. Namely, I want to thank the academic dean of the faculty during my participation in and writing of this project, Dr. Leah Gunning Francis, for her unwavering support of me and my vocational growth and well-being and president David Mellott for his ready encouragement and steady leadership through out this process as well. I am also grateful for the formative educational experience I received at Emory University and the Candler School of Theology. I stand on the shoulders of so many professors and mentors whose guidance and mentorship helped me develop as a pastoral theologian and in my craft as a psychotherapist.

Many thanks to my colleague and coauthor, Rev. Tim Shapiro. It has been a joy to learn with and from you as we have journeyed through curating and leading each cohort of the Formative Power project. You represent one of the most heart-led, authentic, and effective leaders I have had the privilege of working with. Thank you for that privilege.

Finally, I remain deeply grateful for the support and inspiration of my husband, Ryan, and children, Madison and Carter, and for all the ways they make this life full of wonder, joy, love, soccer games, carpools, and grace—so much grace.

Acknowledgments

I (Tim) acknowledge how churches have been a prime agent in my lifelong, never-ending desire for spiritual growth. These churches include Northminster Presbyterian Church; Second Presbyterian Church of Indianapolis; Bethlehem Presbyterian Church in Logansport, Indiana; and Westminster Presbyterian Church in Xenia, Ohio. I also lift with thanks Geneva Center Camp and Conference Center, an extension of congregational life. I am grateful for its leader in the 1980s, the Rev. Ken Watt.

The church isn't the only school for life. So are colleges, universities, and seminaries. Every day, I am reminded of what I've been taught at Purdue University and Louisville Presbyterian Theological Seminary.

The idea of the *Formative Power of Your Congregation* is linked to many clergy and theologians, but none more so than Dr. Craig Dykstra. Though the contents of this book are from Christina's and my perspectives, the idea and the title, or better yet, the reality, originally came from Dr. Dykstra, particularly his book *Growing in the Life of Faith*.

This volume wouldn't exist without the generous support of Lilly Endowment, Inc. whose sole funding made both the Formative Program and the Center for Congregations in Indiana possible. We are deeply grateful to Dr. Chris Coble, their vice president of Religion, for his invaluable guidance on the Formative Program and across all Center initiatives.

Many dedicated colleagues at the Center contributed to the Formative endeavor. Kelly Minas, our program evaluator, greatly enhanced the experience. The Center is truly a one-of-a-kind organization in the United States, and I am honored to be a part of this remarkable community.

The Center for Congregations supports two outstanding seminaries: Christian Theological Seminary and Louisville Presbyterian Theological Seminary.

Board members at the time this manuscript was submitted represent leadership at its best: Dr. Richard Hamm, Elizabeth Clay, Colleen Kenney, Dr. David Mellott, Dr. Andrew Pomerville, Rev. Michael Jefferson, Rev. Lynn Martin, Charlitta Winston, Rev. Annettra Jones, Ted Waggoner, and Rev. Javier Mondragon. Special mention goes to Dr. William Kincaid, Dr. Alton Pollard, and Katherine Patterson.

I return to the phrase "a great cloud of witnesses" (Hebrews 12:1). Those in that cloud who have moved ever so powerfully and gently with me include Zander Grashow, Dr. William L. Steele (quoted at length in the book), Dr. William Enright, Dr. Johanna Bos, Dr. John McClure, Dr. Amy Plantinga Pauw, Dr. James Rafferty, Dr. Thomas Schweinberg, Dr. Lorene Walter, and Dr. Elizabeth Mariutto.

Writing a book with Dr. Christina Jones Davis was a pleasure and more than that too. From you, Christina, I experienced insightful perspectives and gentle nudges encouraging growth. You possess an intuitive understanding of human experience, offering guidance with such sensitivity and wisdom. Thank you.

I have been called to and allowed to serve two blessed congregations, the two named above—Bethlehem and Westminster Presbyterian. Some congregants who represent what was good and right about the whole include Bill Freshour, Betty Davidson, Jane Howard, Dan and Pat Reef, Buzz Reed, Harold and Marilyn Hanlin, Essie Payne, Elaine and John Grayson, and Connie and Michael Hunter. Through them and many others, I know the meaning of "saint."

My immediate family is dazzling. They are also quiet and made uncomfortable by spotlights. So I run past the superlatives but pause to say "Love wins!" to Gretchen, Jacob, Ian, and Eli.

We also want to thank our wonderfully supportive partners at Alban Books, Anna Keyser, Victoria Shi, Dr. Richard Brown, our peer-review readers, and the entire publication team. We are thankful you saw the value of our work and helped us share it with the world. We extend words of gratitude to our editor, Sarah Brown, who was a source of both the calm and the correction necessary to ready our writing for the printed page.

Last but not least, we thank you, our readers. Thank you for lending us your attention and trusting us with your curiosity that has brought you this far. Our hope and prayer is for you, and your congregation, to be nourished by something we (or the Spirit) say such that you will grow, flourish, and be well.

Ashe and may it be so.[1]

NOTE

1. Velma E. Love, *Divining the Self: A Study in Yoruba Myth and Human Consciousness* (University Park: Pennsylvania State University Press, 2012), 55.

Introduction

Simply, or not simply, operating a church requires people who contribute to its day-to-day operations. Clergy and laity work to keep the building safe, the sanctuary warm, the lawn green, and the carpet clean. You may lead the nominating committee for officers. Someone serves as treasurer. Another makes sure parishioners have paper plates for fellowship hour. You may have been part of a strategic planning team or considered how much to give the capital campaign effort. Yes, there is much to do in a congregation.

Yet the congregation you attend is potentially more powerful than you know. Remember why your congregation was important to you in the first place? Who among us participates in congregational life with the highest aspiration being to make sure there is fresh ice in their congregation's kitchen?

Under the night sky, we, all of us, feel definitively small. Whether it is lights of the city or the light of the stars, we wonder if what we do day to day matters. Yet, however great the expanse of creation, who we are makes a difference. Our lives are made to have purpose. We are created to benefit the entire universe for God's sake. A woman who teaches fifth grade in the public schools says, "When I was in high school, my Sunday school teacher ended class the same way every week. It was like her benediction: *'Now, go and remember that whatever happens to one of us happens to all of us.'*" Twenty years on, this public school teacher ends her Friday classes with these same words for her students.

Who we are matters and, for many of us, church has formed us benediction after benediction.

The Formative Power of Your Congregation activities serve as a primary catalyst for your human development. Different life factors shape who you are. Certainly, various features of your life contribute to the meaning you make of life. Many elements support your development as a human being (and sometimes they detract). Of course, parents pass along a design of genetic material just as our parents received from their parents. Yes, an abundance of factors determine the you that is you. These factors include past experiences, racial or ethnic identity, gender, vocation, geography, relationships, decisions, education, and more. We explore these multiple factors further in chapter 4.

Your participation in a congregation also forms who you are. Whether apparent or hidden, your congregation shapes how you make meaning. Your faith community develops not only your faith but also your life (as if religion could be separate from life). You study the Sermon on the Mount as remembered by Matthew (5:9). You read, "Blessed are the peacemakers, for they will be called children of God." You receive this proclamation soul deep. A few months later, you begin serving as a volunteer facilitator for the family court, working with youth attending a class as an alternative to suspension from the family court program. As you work with these youth, you become fond of them and empathetic to their challenges. Over time, you and the youth are peacemaking even if you don't call it that. Together, you are treating one another as children of God even if you don't directly connect this sense with the Matthew passage. You find yourself loving (yes, loving) these students who were strangers three months before. Was the Matthew passage the only contributor to your experience? No, most likely not. Yet the relationship between Scripture and being with the students is formed, consciously or not, by your experience with Scripture in your congregation.

Matters of Christian formation and spiritual growth are often cited as among the essential aims of congregational life. Yet volunteering in a family court program or knowing that what you do every day affects others is a qualitatively different view of Christian formation or spiritual growth. Formation isn't exclusively an in-church term. Our congregation, at its best, forms who we are (at our best) beyond the contours of congregational life. Our congregation forms who we are—heart, mind, and strength—as we participate in the geography of day-to-day life.

FRAMEWORK

This book shows how our lives are formed throughout our existence, but particularly by congregational practices for the sake of our participation in God's aims beyond the doors of the church. What you will read about in this book has developed as we taught and learned from forty Indiana congregations.

We referenced a three-part framework that intersects in such a way that human development occurs and is applied. This three-part framework is based on the hypothesis that our growth involves three elements. First, where we live and have our being is the playing field of life. There would be no reason to care about human development if it had no bearing on our day-to-day activity and identity. Second, we chose the congregation as the means of formation because, frankly, we value congregational life and beliefs, and we believe that congregations' primary reason for being is human development, not the confirmation of an institution. Finally, we provided the rationale for what we called trail markers (more detail to follow). For now, know that we chose what we are calling trail markers because they parallel many of the signifiers of human development used in a variety of fields. Therefore, insights from human development, also known as developmental psychology, provide an essential lens through which we understand how humans are formed throughout life, and particularly in congregations.

Therefore, the framework contains three parts:

- life arenas
- congregational practices
- trail markers

People live in various arenas, where human development and spiritual growth extend beyond the sanctuary's confines. The application of human development and spiritual formation doesn't stop at the sanctuary door. We define a life arena as an experience that holds value to a person, a part of life where one wants to develop responsibility for the wellness of their soul, ultimately leading to deeper connections with others. Life arenas are the different areas of our lives where we find meaning and purpose. They may include our family, our vocation, our finances, our wellness, the arts, education, and social justice. When we are intentional about our spiritual growth in these areas, we can experience a deeper sense of connection with ourselves, others, and God. Life arenas include:

- *Family:* Our relationships with family members let us practice love and forgiveness.
- *Vocation:* Our work can give life meaning and help us nurture our talents.
- *Finances:* Money can teach us about generosity and financial responsibility.
- *Wellness:* Taking care of our physical and mental health is vital for our well-being.
- *The arts:* Creative outlets allow us to express ourselves artistically.
- *Education:* Learning helps us understand the world and develop critical thinking skills, while also deepening our faith.
- *Social justice:* Issues like racism and economic injustice inspire us to strive for a fairer, more suitable world.

The Formative Power of Your Congregation participants named and defined these life arenas. We provided examples, but participants identified the life arenas most important to them.

In these settings, practicing the faith includes unique and varied expressions of essential, deeply rooted activities done by people who seek to thoughtfully, actively, and competently embody the way of Christ with and for others.

The second part of the framework includes congregational practices. Such practices include worship and all its elements, including prayer, sermons, offerings, music, and more. Congregational experiences include retreats, pilgrimages, moments of transcendence, and the care of souls. Each congregation is unique, so a congregational practice in one assembly may not exist or might take a different form in another. Congregations, even from the same movement, are not franchises like McDonald's. Have you noticed that whether you walk into a McDonald's in San Diego or one in Philadelphia, the experience is almost identical? Not so with churches. Congregational practices such as sermons and Bible studies are standard but vary significantly among assemblies. Often, those aspects that are distinctive to a particular congregation are the most powerful. "What happens to one of us happens to all of us" is not found in a denomination's book of prayers. Yet, as repeated in this church every Sunday, it was vital to forming those present. Congregational practices shape a life where one is developing into one's best self, growth represented by a sudden epiphany or growth subtle and seeded quietly in the soul.

HUMAN DEVELOPMENT

We were not sure, at first, how our list of trail markers should represent virtue. Classically, Christian virtue is defined as representing the fruit of the Holy Spirit: love, joy, peace, patience, kindness, goodness, faithfulness, gentleness, and self-control (Galatians 5:25–26). Such virtues are positive attributes. However, the word "virtue," in some settings, represents a binary separation of good and bad. You either possess good character or bad character. You are either virtuous or you are not.

That wouldn't do.

So we decided that trail markers should signify human development. Our choice to use the framework of human development demonstrates our desire to match formation with growth rather than with a static designation of good character or bad character.

The discipline of human development (both the study of and the actual experience of development) accounts for an inner shift that results in growth in how you relate to others, how you experience God, how you find your voice, and how you come to know your influence on others and others' influence on you. Some of the human development language we apply is often used by mental health practitioners. Even though we strongly affirm growth that occurs through therapy, we apply the markers related to growth that can be traced back to congregational life. Such markers include attachment, self-differentiation, authority, competence, integration, and emotional regulation.

WHY THIS BOOK MATTERS TO US

When I (Tim) was in high school, my widowed mother married a widower. So I was living in a blended family (comparing my family to the Brady Bunch reveals my age). In a family of seven, in which half of the family was new to me, I didn't talk much, knowing that even when I was correct, my stepfather—a resilient man who lived in the lack-of-oxygen environment of abusive poverty—would correct me as being wrong.

I went to church. I lived for Sunday evenings and youth group. When I was sixteen, I was one of several peers who led the 7 p.m. Christmas Eve service.

I practiced my part (which I had written). I stood on the chancel steps and spoke. The Rev. Verne Sindlinger positioned himself at the back of the sanctuary. Each time I delivered my teenage homily, Rev. Sindlinger would forcefully say back to me, "Speak louder." Four times. "Speak louder": an invitation in contrast to my voice not subjectively mattering at home. Did my pastor know what he was doing? Maybe or maybe not. Years later, I know its effect. Each time I was told to speak louder, something inside me shifted, an inner voice, shaping a sense of authority (my words have consequence, for good and for bad) and competence. I can do this. In fact, I'm good at speaking in front of others, an important skill for a preacher.

When I think of the formative power of the congregation, I (Christina) think about a church in rural east Texas my family has been a part of for many generations that was established in 1874. It started at a family farm to provide spiritual support, community, outreach, and hope during the tumultuous Reconstruction era after the Civil War. Over time, but not initially, this community built a sanctuary in which it gathered the already formed members of a congregation, a congregation whose descendants would go on to profoundly shape my own development.

As a painfully shy preschool-age girl, it was within this congregation that I first stood in the pulpit in front of dozens of reassuring faces to recite my Easter poem each year, long before I experienced a call to preach from that same pulpit. It is also where I sang shoulder to shoulder (or shoulder to leg in my youth) and danced with my elders on land where my ancestors were once enslaved. Looking back, I now see how the act of singing, clapping, stomping, and dancing alongside loved ones was, and still is, a deeply anchoring, healing, and transcendent formative experience. As an adult, I can testify to how vital these experiences were to key developmental tasks and that these formative experiences were both personal and communal, both unique and common.

All or most of us grow, or we stumble, or we try to keep ourselves from stumbling. Craig Dykstra notes, "Faith means freedom, the freedom at last to give up the anxious and impossible task of keeping oneself from falling."[1] Martin Buber writes, "All real life is meeting."[2] So goes, "All real life is growing." Yet the trail of our years is not a contest. I fix you; you fix me. No. What is at stake is your congregation's energy to assist your growth into a life in which what happens to you, what you make happen, happens to all of us. Such a claim testifies to the unbounded presence of God at work in the space between you and me. Such a claim testifies to the importance of who we are under the immense canopy of a night sky, and to the unbounded presence of God remarkably active in the formative power of congregations. You and I may not attain the full measure of Christ (did the writer of Ephesians 4 mean this in any way other than aspirational?). Yet, through imperfect and good enough (both) congregational practices, you and I develop in such a way that we can address, rather than shirk, the ever-increasing demands of life, making meaning and living for the sake of God's creation.

THE PRIMARY PURPOSE OF CONGREGATIONS

This book came to be because we witnessed, repeatedly, congregational leaders who (without intending to or realizing it) had forgotten—or had otherwise gotten distracted by institutional maintenance to-do lists—the primary purpose of a congregation. Some religious worldviews proclaim that a congregation's primary purpose is as a mediator of individual salvation. Another view is that the congregation provides a course for sanctification and growth in Christlikeness. Still another view is that congregations exist to speak truth to power for the sake of God's realm. All these views, in particular contexts, contain meaning making for adherents.

We have written this book as a distillation of a variety of ecclesiologies. What are congregations for? God's purpose for your congregation is not growth—it's the development of human beings and the flourishing of the local community.

From this conviction, we learned how certain congregations immerse adherents in formative activities that relate directly to what matters most to them as they move—day to day—through life.

As theological educators, we often meet others when they are bright-eyed about their ministries, carrying a sense of call and purpose sustainable for them and their communities. It is well known that burnout in ministry is not uncommon and often occurs within the first five years.[3] While religious belief is often considered a protective factor against burnout, a powerfully formative congregation may be a vital and often overlooked factor as well. This book is an effort to chart pathways of well-being for clergy and congregations alike, because not only do well leaders often make for well congregations, but well congregations help their leaders sustain wellness in turn.

REAL-LIFE EXAMPLES

Our hypothesis is that nobody chooses (or is it called?) to attach to a congregation because she wants to be a volunteer for the institution called "church."

Imagine a congregation that sponsors what is called a "Life Group" on Thursday nights. The purpose of the Life Group is for young adults to listen into being (that's what the leader calls the conversations). The young adults share stories, test dreams, and care for one another as they discern what they most want to do in the next five years. Each group begins with one person (alternating readers at each gathering) reading the same Bible passage each week: 1 John 4:7: "Beloved, let us love one another, for love is from God, and whoever loves has been born of God and knows God."

Every meeting ends with the group reciting the Lord's Prayer together.

"My task on Sunday morning is to visit every Sunday school class and count attendance," the facilitator says. "That's not going to help me decide if God is calling me to medicine or to social work." So she started the Life Group.

Some congregants experience or perceive faith communities as only attending to church life, as if the everyday is not a landscape for that which is spiritual. Why so binary? This project views congregations as places to grow as people such that they live more full, abundant, and well lives. In many ways, the impact of the COVID-19 pandemic (not unlike pandemics our ancestors experienced) reminded us of all our human fragility. Faith communities developed practices around the proximity and fragility of bodies in an effort to support the wellness of those bodies. The same is true for other areas of wellness. While such matters are not always discussed, congregants experience day-to-day pressures and experiences they bring with them to their faith communities. What would it mean if we did more to acknowledge the whole life of the congregant and, even more, support their formation in ways that improved their overall well-being in life? The congregation becomes a school for life rather than a volunteer society to keep the institution running.

One may notice that we do not set out to narrowly define what whole-person wellness is, as we recognize that wellness and formation are contextual—that is, we are being formed by our various neighborhoods, cultures, families from birth, etc., and congregations are often a reflection of these contexts in some way.

BEYOND PRACTICAL

The origin of this project came from observing congregations that, for heaven's sake, make a mission out of life. We observed vital congregations move from a volunteer-based organization seeking growth or survival to one of the primary places where people learn to be the simple yet multidimensional phrase: more human.

A generation ago, essayist (farmer, novelist, and poet) Wendell Berry wrote a book titled *What Are People For?*[4]

This project is a response to the question, "What are congregations for?"

Much of the book's content comes from our experience with congregations participating in a program of the Center for Congregations (in Indiana), The Formative Power of Your Congregation.[5] The Center for Congregations is funded by Lilly Endowment and is a supporting organization of two theological schools: Christian Theological Seminary and Louisville Presbyterian Theological Seminary. All these organizations form adults in various theological attitudes. For many years, the Center for Congregations has responded to congregational requests (or presenting issues) such as fundraising, building assessments, demographic studies, and the training of volunteers.

The Center for Congregations' early mission statement reads: "The Center for Congregations strengthens congregations by helping them address their practical challenges." All those practical functions, and more, are real issues that need attention. And yet, theological schools (and the Center for Congregations) want more. Indeed, one of the many good things that happen at a theological school is the formation of an individual as part of a community—the seminary community. Picture the disappointment when seminary graduates, who know their purpose is to help God and communities change lives, find that most of their time involves fundraising or building repair. Such activities can be done but are not inherently formative. For example, what if congregations form members in financial literacy or entrepreneurship while fundraising? And what if congregations invited the handiest and craftiest of people to repair and refurbish the building alongside those who wish to learn the skills and artistry involved?

A growing number of congregational leaders seek more than practical advice from the Center for Congregations. Fewer clergy and laity contacted the Center for resources about, say, how to trade pews for chairs. More congregations (still a minority) seek resources about arenas more essential to a life well lived. *Do you know a counselor to talk with us about trauma? Who would be a good guest speaker, one who would challenge us, about racism? Our parents are overwhelmed. What can the church do?*

THE FORMATIVE PROCESS

Much of this book is shaped by the multiyear Formative Power of Your Congregation educational experience sponsored by the Center for Congregations in Indiana. The authors of this book developed the curriculum. The overarching learning goal is for congregations to design and then undertake a learning journey that supports human development through the power of congregational practices and the experience of a life arena important to congregants.

All participating congregations were from Indiana. Most participating congregations represented BIPOC assemblies. Four learning cohorts were formed with an average of ten participating congregations each. Each congregation formed a formative team that participated in four workshops. During the process, congregations received grant funds to experiment with their formation idea. After the fourth class, congregations were invited to apply for a grant that would fund their work.

As described above, the curriculum focused on three areas, which we called congregational practices, life arenas, and trail markers.

Each congregation was asked to decide, through a discernment process, about a part of life (life arena) upon which adherents would focus. Vocation, antiracism, creation care, household finances, the arts, family life, and equity in the neighborhood are examples of the kind of life arenas congregations chose.

Juxtaposed with life arenas were congregational practices. Such practices include prayer, worship, Bible study, religious education, pilgrimages, retreats, local mission, and more. How might congregational practices support the chosen life arena?

The desired result was that congregants would experience personal growth as a result of the energy emerging from the juxtaposition of the life arena with congregational practices. The markers (trail markers) of personal growth include aspects of character attributed to the realm of human development and/or religious commitments.

Participating in congregational life is less about joining and more about being. This connection provides us with a sense of belonging that connects our soul to a larger purpose: the ultimate aim of personal development and our contribution to the community beyond ourselves. The wager is that this is what we seek if we only knew how. Congregations as a formative power lead people to a life congruent with their religious claims and commitments. A family, a workplace, a neighborhood, or a school all have the power to sculpt people into particular ways of life. So do congregations as imperfect assemblies of always-being-refined human beings.

David Cunningham argues that belonging results in more than being known by the company you keep. He states that "you gradually become the company you keep."[6] He writes, "Over time, the stories that those other people live by, and the practices in which they are engaged, will become your stories and your practices as well. And your character will be formed by those habits, just as surely as theirs have been."

David Cunningham's quote suggests that belonging goes beyond mere association with a particular group; it implies a transformative influence on an individual.

So, yes, a Sunday school teacher ends each session by saying, *"Now, go and remember that whatever happens to one of us happens to all of us."*

Twenty years later, a class member repeats the same words to her public school students.

The practices and stories of the congregation you belong to become a part of your narrative and behavior. It's not just a matter of external recognition; it's an internalization of the collective identity and habits of the assembly. Over time, these shared stories and practices shape your character, molding it into alignment with, hopefully, the highest habits and values of your faith community.

And there's more. Congregations not only can increase a person's impact in an area of life; they are also temples of meaning making:

- Who am I?
- What am I here for?
- Where am I headed?

Congregations are deeply felt public places where people come together to build a deeper understanding of life's meaning via shared practices. Such shared practices help individuals interpret their existence and feel a sense of belonging beyond their immediate social circle. So, being part of a congregation shapes who we are and contributes to a shared sense of purpose for everyone involved.

Some congregations' buildings may be downtown, near a field, or in a school (even online?). Regardless, above are the stars of an unfathomably vast universe, and underneath the immense night sky our lives might feel small but they are not diminished. Over time, perhaps unpredictably, this sometimes improbable community called a congregation has made our lives dynamic and transformed them in beautiful and unexpected ways.

What was it that Howard Thurman said?

"Don't ask yourself what the world needs. Ask yourself what makes you come alive, and go do that, because what the world needs is people who have come alive."[7]

How does your congregation harness the power to form healthy and thriving human beings who are fully alive? This book aims to support those who serve, lead, and otherwise join with congregational life in ways that are deeply and powerfully formative.

QUESTIONS FOR REFLECTION

1. Ultimately, what do you think congregations are for?
2. Identify one of the ways a church formed some aspect of who you are.
3. How is that aspect of formation important to your day-to-day life?

NOTES

1. Craig Dykstra, *Growing in the Life of Faith: Education and Christian Practices* (Louisville: Westminster John Knox Press, 1999), 21.
2. Martin Buber, *I and Thou* (Edinburgh: T&T Clark, 1923), 11.
3. A 2013 study from the Schaeffer Institute reports that 1,700 pastors leave the ministry each month, citing depression, burnout, or being overworked as the primary reasons. According to the study, 90 percent of pastors report working fifty-five to seventy hours a week, and 50 percent of them feel unable to meet the demands of the job. However, some studies suggest that clergy burn out at a lesser rate than many other helping professions, such as Christopher J. Adams, Holly Hough, Rae Jean Proeschold-Bell, Jia Yao, and Melanie Kolkin, "Clergy Burnout: A Comparison Study with Other Helping Professions," *Pastoral Psychology* 66 (July 2016): 147–75.
4. Wendell Berry, *What Are People For?* (San Francisco: North Point Press, 1990).
5. Dykstra, *Growing in the Life of Faith*. The title comes from Craig Dykstra, who asserts that congregations not only give shape to the quality and character of the lives of people; they do so in community, not in isolation.
6. David Cunningham, *Christian Ethics: The End of the Law* (New York: Routledge, 2008), 39.
7. Howard Thurman, quoted in Gil Bailie, *Violence Unveiled: Humanity at the Crossroads* (New York: Crossroad, 1995), xv. Gil Bailie tells this story in

the first paragraph of the "In Gratitude" section of his book: "Once, when I was seeking the advice of Howard Thurman and talking to him at some length about what needed to be done in the world, he interrupted me and said, 'Don't ask yourself what the world needs. Ask yourself what makes you come alive, and go do that, because what the world needs is people who have come alive.'" This is the only known print location of this quote.

PART I

Conceptual Understandings and the Curriculum Framework

Chapter 1

A Contextual Theology of Congregational Life

What is a church for? A recent survey of priests and pastors revealed answers to this very question.[1]

For the pastor of a Catholic church located on Chicago's South Side that has been nationally recognized for commitment to equality and passionate stances against racism, injustice, and gun violence:

> Church must be the place where we gather to be healed, loved and strengthened, but also challenged and trained to impact the world.
> For the pastor of an intergenerational Christian Reformed congregation on the campus of a large university:
> The church is called to gather disciples, and continue forming them into a community of mutual service.

For a pastor in Portland, Oregon, of a multiethnic congregation that is theologically conservative but politically all over the map and learning how to live together in a national culture that is becoming increasingly polarized and divisive:

> We are to be a place of heaven breaking into earth.
> For the pastor of a predominantly African American evangelical congregation in Madison, Wisconsin:
> Church is for all people!

For an ordained pastor in the Communion of Reformed Evangelical Churches (CREC) who has served in pastorates in Alabama and Idaho:

The church exists as the community of that future feast, an outpost of the world to come in this world.

The church is for many things. The diversity of responses points not only to the many things church is for, but to the many people *who* the church is. The church is comprised of people, and people are inescapably contextualized. So then is our theology of congregational life. The curriculum presented in this book privileges the contextual, lived experiences of congregations of people and the power therein. We opted for the term "congregational life" rather than "church" to capture what we are theologizing and to highlight and emphasize the dynamism of the real, messy, beautiful, and day-to-day lives of those who constitute the church.

It is also the case that we, as curators of this project, are embedded within contexts as well. We have had our own formative experiences in congregations that we reflected on early and often throughout this project. Additionally, the fields of ecclesiology and practical theology have deeply shaped us vocationally—one of us a pastor and a multi-congregation organizational leader for many years and one a theology professor and marriage and family therapist. Both of us have studied these disciplines for our doctoral work. We seek to helpfully draw upon these fields of study to help us define what we mean by "a theology of congregational life."

We decided to explicitly outline the influence of these disciplines at the outset of our book for a few reasons. First, they were the lenses, both consciously and unconsciously, that guided the design and much of the meaning making that formed this project. Second, ecclesiology and practical theology offer sets of frameworks, language, and concepts for helping us understand just how and why congregations form people.

We hope the discussion in this chapter will provide orienting theological themes and concepts of both ecclesiology and practical theology on which forthcoming chapters will build. We will begin by defining and exploring what ecclesiology is and how it undergirds our statements about the power of congregations, as we considered this most foundational. We will then turn to pastoral theology as a way of expanding the congregational practices integral to this project. Let's begin with our ecclesiology.

A CONTEXTUAL ECCLESIOLOGY

Ecclesiology was, in part, born out of a historical need for the church to define and differentiate itself.[2] Whether it be a church differentiating itself from those who are nonreligious, those who are of different faiths, or those with varying perspectives within the faith, self-definition is an ongoing process. Differentiation is in many ways just as important to institutions as it is to individuals in matters of developing and maintaining an identity.

Those who were involved in ecclesiological dialogues, such as those of the Second Vatican Council between 1962 and 1965, included Catholic and Protestant leaders and laypersons.[3] This gathering did not include all who made up the church then or now. Namely, women and persons of color who now constitute the majority of the global church were not well represented in these definitional discussions.[4] Those like Rosemary Radford Reuther, one of the pioneers of feminist ecclesiology, have critiqued the exclusive focus of church as institution and urge us not to simply ask what the church is but *who* is the church. As such, the study and definitions of ecclesiology have become more inclusive and multivocal since its origins.

Fundamentally, the word "ecclesiology" itself comes from the Greek word *ecclesia* meaning "assembly." It is the power of this living—and lively—assembly we call a congregation that we wager impacts human formation in ways worth looking at more closely and enacting more intentionally (but more on this later). It is our view that ecclesiology is always contextual, and the ways of understanding the nature of this assembly of persons are multiple rather than singular. Comparative ecclesiology as a methodology affirms this variety by developing approaches of systematic reflection between the many different ecclesiologies.[5] Forms of comparative ecclesiology often proceed along a spectrum—objective comparisons, followed by ecumenical dialogue and analysis, and finally interreligious comparisons with other religious communities.[6]

One can also appreciate the multivalence of ecclesiology through the numerous biblical images and symbols that have operated as definitional for congregations. For example, biblical texts that describe the church as the temple of the Spirit, the body of Christ, the kingdom of God, or the people of God attest to the multiple expressions of what and who the church is.[7] With such a plethora of ways to talk about one's ecclesiology, you, having picked up this book, are almost certainly most interested in what exactly *we* mean by ecclesiology within our context(s).

For our work with the Formative Power of Your Congregation project, we have defined ecclesiology as a discipline that examines a congregation's *beliefs*, *identity*, and *activity*. Moreover, we are interested in the formative power a congregation's beliefs, identity, and activity have on shaping the individuals who comprise it. In many ways, all three aspects of who the church is go hand in hand in a dynamic interplay of influence. Beliefs impact identity, out of which flows certain activities, which then can further shape beliefs, as seen in figure 1.1.

Let us first discuss how beliefs and identity are connected and integral to our theology of congregational life. We will then explore how practical theology assists us with the outgrowth of activities that follow.

For most congregations, a shared belief system, or faith tradition, is the starting point. And for those identifying as Christian congregations, it is often the common faith and understanding of the Gospel of Jesus Christ. This shared belief provides a framework for understanding the world and one's place and purpose within it. This shared faith also, in turn, shapes the identity and activities of that same assembly. As theologian Stanley Hauerwas writes, "the church is not simply a group of people who happen to believe certain things; it is a community of people whose belief in turn shapes their lives and their identity as

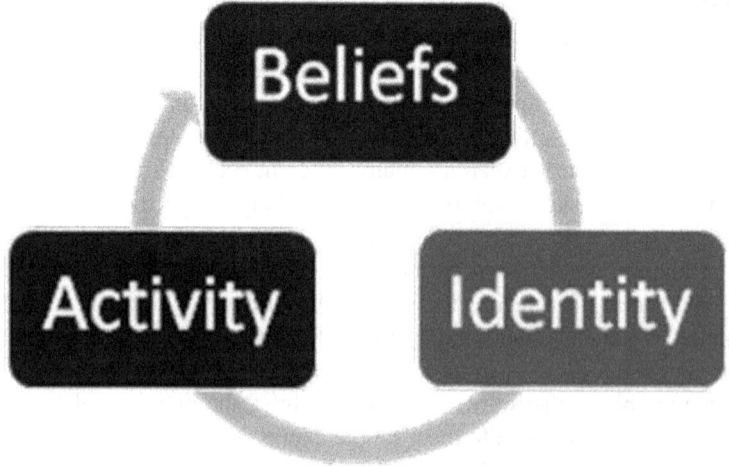

Figure 1.1. Ecclesiological Circle

people."[8] For example, in some congregations the Trinity anchors the understanding of the church as one of communion or koinonia in the shared life of God, who is relational. This belief in a relational God can shape the way persons understand relationship to self, one another, and the communities around them.[9] From the belief that God is relational, congregations may engage the activities of gathering regularly on both Wednesdays and Sundays, make efforts to be neighbors in their sanctuary community and neighborhoods, and enact practices and programs that seek to include and connect with those who otherwise feel left out or forgotten. Take for instance the congregation that we worked with started hosting community dinners that invited its membership and wider community to share in a meal each week as an expression of this relational belief. Figure 1.2 shows this feedback loop.

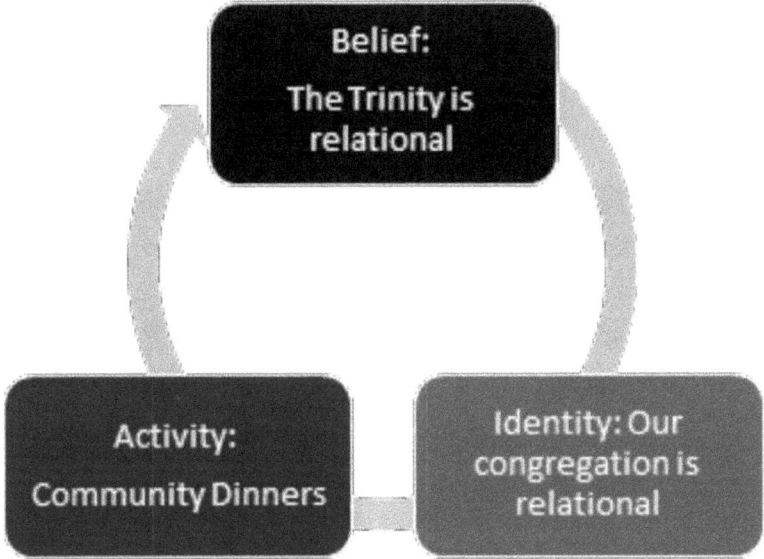

Figure 1.2. Ecclesiological Circle Example

Another example of how a congregation's beliefs profoundly impact its sense of identity and activity relates to the belief of belonging to the body of Christ among congregants. Belonging to a local religious community shapes individuals' self-identification as well as the belief in a larger, global Christian body. This sense of belonging provides a framework for personal and communal identity formation as well.

Congregants see themselves as members of the body of Christ, which influences their understanding of themselves as interconnected members of the world.[10] In such cases, congregants may be inclined to do what one congregation we worked with did by partnering with their neighborhood school to volunteer in the library and lead youth book clubs. They did so because their belief in interconnectedness with others did not get truncated at the threshold of the church doors; it extended into the world around them. Figure 1.3 demonstrates this flow.

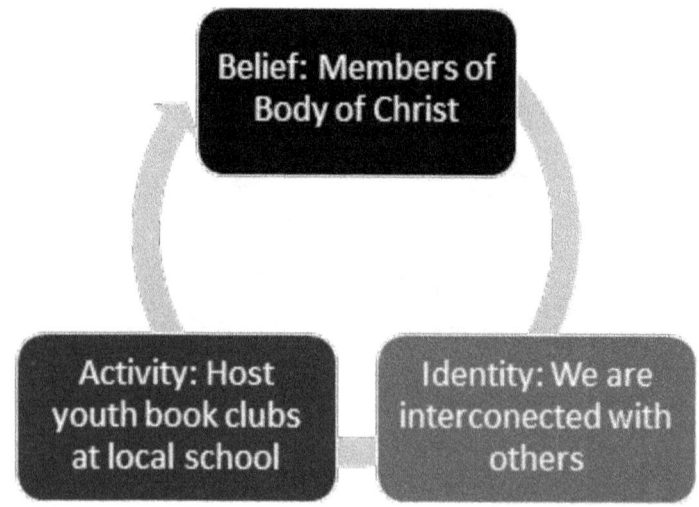

Figure 1.3. Ecclesiological Circle Example

Hopefully we have demonstrated how our approach to ecclesiology provides a framework for considering more closely how a congregation's beliefs connect to matters of identity and lead to the outgrowth of certain activities. While the aspiration is often for all three of these elements of the ecclesiological circle to align, all congregations experience some dissonance between an espoused ecclesial belief, a particular held identity, and actions that follow. Acknowledging this reality makes the spaces between belief, identity, and action a necessarily ongoing dialogical exchange. We do not arrive; we can only commit to allowing the interrogation of the Spirit and accountability of fellow human beings to bring about greater alignment.

Now that we have defined and described the three core elements that constitute our ecclesiology, we will expound on an area of great significance to our project—the activity of congregations. To build further upon the activity of congregations, we turn to practical theology. As a discipline, practical theology is especially assistive in understanding both the activity of the church and those who participate in and shape this activity.

A CONTEXTUAL PRACTICAL THEOLOGY

Practical theology is a field that has been traditionally interdisciplinary, which in ways makes an all-encompassing definition for the field less helpful than looking at the areas that constitute it. One area of practical theology is pastoral theology, which is a discipline concerned with theologies, theories, and practices of pastoring. Drilling down further, the practical, skill-based arena of pastoral theology is often referred to as pastoral care. Pastoral care includes the study of the nature of skills, character, and formation that enable effectiveness and non-harming in various ministry roles. While distinct in some ways, categories and definitions within practical theology are often diffuse and overlapping, as seen in figure 1.4.[11]

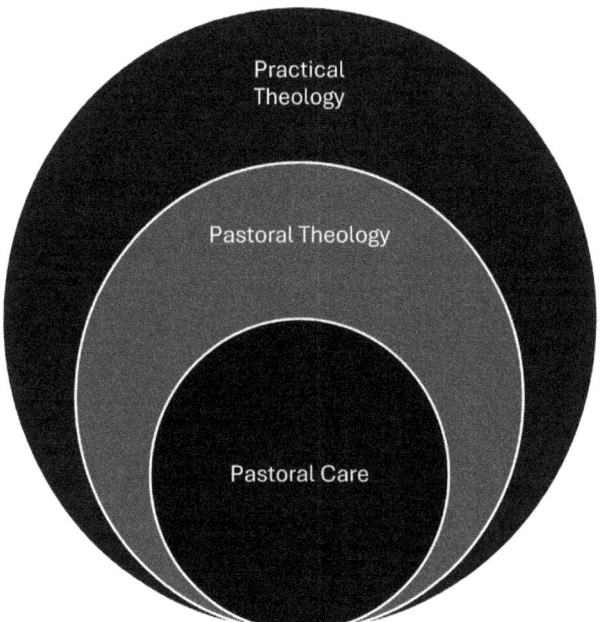

Figure 1.4. Practical Theology Areas

While pastoral theology and pastoral care are aspects of practical theology, our project is chiefly concerned with a broader application of practical theology. This kind of practical theology can be defined as reflection on our participation in and with the emergence and maintenance of communities of authentic transformation in the world.[12] Practical theology enables a community to reflect upon and guide its own action in the context of God's continuing action.

In this project, the social sciences as an aspect of practical theology also inform our reflections on the practices of ministry.[13] We employ the social science of human development, or developmental psychology, which seeks to describe predicable patterns of psychological and relational changes as one grows and matures from birth to death. We explore how communities of faith are environments that are a powerful source of authentic formation and transformation of human beings. In doing this, we are practicing our own practical theological methodology.

Practical theology is also about *how* theology is done.[14] The term "pastoral" when used to refer to aspects of practical theology simultaneously means "accountable to" a community of faith.[15] Practical theology is, for us, a way of doing theology that is accountable to communities, particularly the contingent of communities with whom we had the opportunity to partner over the course of this project. While working with forty faith communities, how have we sought to hold ourselves accountable to them all?

Within the last half century, much attention has been given to the development of pastoral theology so that it better comes to terms with the complexities of a postmodern world. As a result, it has duly widened its focus to consider the social, cultural, and political influences on those we serve and ourselves.[16] Despite these developments, it would be erroneous to assume that practical theology as a discipline has now arrived at a state of absolute inclusivity. Nonetheless, our objective has been to hold ourselves accountable to these congregations by employing a contextual approach to practical theology that, when applied, considers the particularities of communities.

WOMANIST THEOLOGY: A MODEL OF CONTEXTUAL, PRACTICAL THEOLOGY

Maintaining a contextual theological lens is inspired by ways of theologizing that are committed to honoring particularity. One methodology we drew upon to shape our approach to practical theology was womanist theology. The origins of womanist theology can be traced back to African American women theologians who were frustrated by both the sexism that was perpetuated in Black liberation theology and the issues of race that had gone unaddressed in feminist thought sought to address the distinct threefold oppression of race, gender, and class, which they understood through a theological lens. In doing so, womanist theology sought to integrate all aspects of life into religiosity. Stephanie Mitchem explains that womanist theology is a theology that must come from African American women's lives to be useful and that these everyday lived experiences are seen as holy.[17] It helps to understand this already well-laid foundation that informs our approach to contextualized, practical theology while working alongside various congregations during this project.

At its core, womanist theology begins with day-to-day experiences that are ordinary rather than abstract.[18] In this way, it employs individual and collective experience as a valid and primary source for doing theology. As a result, one does not do womanist theology by being Black or a woman but because one possesses a "lived-world struggle."[19] Likewise, our source for doing a contextual practical theology is the everyday lives and struggles of the people who make up congregations.

It follows that the aim of a contextual approach to our practical theology is to honor voices native to congregations and the communities they serve. Honoring the voices of congregations maintains their authority to name their most authentic truths.[20] This manner of agency within congregations is vital to empower the kinds of growth that matter most to the people therein. In a contextual practical theological approach, it is of utmost significance that communities act as agents on their own behalf whenever possible.[21]

In telling and owning one's story, a womanist-oriented practical theology seeks to invoke multiple sources of knowing: one's personal experiences and cultural history, the impact of one's family of origin on one's choice making, and one's responses regarding racism, classism, sexism, heterosexism, and other challenges in this world that impact us all.[22] Importantly, there is no one overarching, monolithic truth or experience. This way of doing theology is inherently both personal and communal as the two are interrelated and necessary to the formation and transformation of self *and* community.[23] The African concept of Ubuntu captures this notion best by reminding us of the interconnectedness of individuals with the community and by affirming that I am because we are, and because we are, I am.[24]

A contextual practical theology was vital when working with the congregations we did in at least three culminating ways. First, it enabled us to address communal needs for survival, wholeness, and liberation by beginning with the experience of the cultures of the congregations versus abstractions about those cultures. Second, it allowed for the significance of community to be held in a creative balance with individuality. And finally, it embraced an expanded view of ministry to include the contributions of all members.[25]

Some might say that our practical theology does not give a detailed enough rubric for the *doing* of contextual practical theology in ways that explicitly define the activity of the church. This is intentional. We would like to think of this approach to a contextual practical theology as most likened to an art form. Contextual practical theologies are an art form that, by their nature, manifest themselves creatively in many different forms. In other words, contextual practical theology cannot and should not be one static form of understanding congregations or partnering with them. It will take on many different forms, while maintaining its integrity. Just like a womanist theology, our methodology is aptly described as musical improvisation. Bearing a strong resemblance to jazz, it uses many instruments—different, individual, improvisational.[26] This sort of methodology helps to foster and protect the most contextually relevant, communally embedded approach to practical theology possible, which we seek not to stifle with manual-like instructions.

We have presented a contextual practical theology based on the principles of womanist theology that seeks to appropriately account for the contextual features of communities with which we partnered. Our method starts with the day-to-day experiences of life and theologically maintains that these everyday experiences are valid sources for doing theology; they are in and of themselves holy. Our hope is that this approach provides a framework that holds us sufficiently accountable to honoring the particularities of each faith community.

A PRACTICAL ECCLESIOLOGY

We have now defined a contextual ecclesiology that examines the church's beliefs, identity, and activity and discussed the formative power of such to shape congregations and congregants alike. We have also engaged practical theology to help further formulate our understanding of congregations both as a means of reflection on our participation in and with the emergence and maintenance of communities of authentic transformation in the world, and as a way of doing theology that is accountable to the communities with which we partner. In doing so, we have drawn upon the wisdom and work of womanist theology that privileges lived experience as a valid source for doing theology.

In the end, there is an imaginative coalescing of ecclesiology and practical theology that emerges in our work, one where contextual ecclesiology joins with practical theology and in turn becomes a *practical ecclesiology*. A practical ecclesiology is concerned with the nature of congregations; the interplay between the beliefs, identity, and ecclesial practices of the church; and how these features relate to the larger world.[27] In other words, the need for a practical ecclesiology is to move beyond the identity of a congregation to how that identity relates and responds to the local sociopolitical situation and the issues therein.[28]

Many of the congregations we worked with were doing just this kind of practical ecclesiology. The connections among belief, identity, and activity in the wider world were evident. Take for instance one congregation we worked with who, from their belief that they are to be good neighbors, embarked on a comprehensive learning experience that included common-ground principles and peacemaking skills learned through a pilgrimage to Israel-Palestine, social events, and the study of Dr. Martin Luther King Jr.'s essay on nonviolence.

Another congregation, to practice their belief in antiracism as necessary to address racism, took a pilgrimage to the California African American Museum, the Martin Luther King Jr. National Historical Park, the Black History and Civil Rights Tour, and the National Museum of African American History and Culture. They saw these activities as shaping their own identity as a multistoried African American community.

A third congregation hoped to empower parishioners to have a lived faith and recognize the call to discipleship within the church and everyday life by focusing on the life arenas of parenting and family life, seeking to strengthen the domestic church through enhanced worship, educational events, small groups, community outreach, retreat experiences, and meals for youth and families to build community within the church and foster a deeper relationship with Jesus Christ.

Together, these congregations illustrate communities that are not only ecclesial but that extend into the public and natural world. Their very identities arise from their contexts and the forces therein.[29] As one can see, the image of the ecclesiological circle within which belief, identity, and activity revolve does not exist in a vacuum but rather through an ongoing exchange of inner and outer mutual influence. A contextual, practical ecclesiology helps us name how this divine dance unfolds.

QUESTIONS FOR REFLECTION

1. What is a story about your congregation that helps you understand its identity?
2. How does the world around you and the day-to-day life of individuals within your congregation shape who your congregation is and what it does?

NOTES

1. "Survey: What Is Church For?" *The Point*, December 15, 2017, https://thepointmag.com/survey/what-is-church-for-pastors (accessed September 2, 2023).

2. Although the term as first employed in a technical sense in the nineteenth century originally referred to the study of church architecture, fabric, and the like, the much broader areas of study encompassed within the subsequent employment of the term have been prominent and prevalent areas of theological enquiry throughout much of the church's existence itself; Gerard Mannion, ed., *Comparative Ecclesiology: Critical Investigations* (London: T&T Clark, 2008).

3. Carroll College, "Vatican II," https://www.carroll.edu/about/history/catholic-history-heritage/vatican-ii (accessed September 2, 2023).

4. Natalie K. Watson, *Introducing Feminist Ecclesiology* (Eugene: Wipf and Stock, 1996).

5. Avery Dulles, *Models of the Church* (New York: Crown, 2002).

6. Roger Haight, "Comparative Ecclesiology," in *The Routledge Companion to the Christian Church*, ed. Gerard Mannion and Lewis S. Mudge, 387–401 (New York: Routledge, 2008).

7. Veli-Matti Kärkkäinen, *An Introduction to Ecclesiology: Historical, Global, and Interreligious Perspectives* (Downers Grove, IL: IVP Academic, 2021), 6–13.

8. Stanley Hauerwas, *Approaching the End: Eschatological Reflections on Church, Politics, and Life* (Grand Rapids, MI: Eerdmans, 2013).

9. Kärkkäinen, *Introduction to Ecclesiology*, 6–13.

10. Vatican Council II, "Lumen Gentium: Dogmatic Constitution on the Church," 1964.

11. Robert C. Dykstra, *Images of Pastoral Care: Classic Readings* (St. Louis: Chalice Press, 2005).

12. Helene Russell and K. Brynolf Lyon, "Positioning Practical Theology: Contextuality, Diversity and Otherness," *Encounter* 72, no. 1 (Spring 2011): 11–30.

13. James Poling, *Foundations for a Practical Theology of Ministry* (Nashville: Abingdon Press, 1985).

14. John Patton, *Pastoral Care in Context: An Introduction to Pastoral Care* (Louisville: Westminster John Knox Press, 1993), 238.

15. Patton, *Pastoral Care in Context*, 242.

16. Nancy Ramsay, *Pastoral Care and Counseling: Redefining Paradigms* (Nashville: Abingdon Press, 2004), 43.

17. Stephanie Y. Mitchem, *Introducing Womanist Theology* (Maryknoll, NY: Orbis, 2002), 58, 77.

18. Carroll A. Watkins Ali, *Survival & Liberation: Pastoral Theology in African American Context* (St. Louis: Chalice Press, 1999), 57.

19. Mitchem, *Introducing Womanist Theology*, 58, 77.

20. Mitchem, *Introducing Womanist Theology*, 24.

21. Mitchem, *Introducing Womanist Theology*, 23.

22. Mitchem, *Introducing Womanist Theology*, 23.

23. Emilie M. Townes, "To Be Called Beloved: Womanist Ontology in Postmodern Refraction," in *Womanist Theological Ethics: A Reader*, ed. Katie Geneva Cannon, Emilie M. Townes, and Angela D. Sims (Louisville: Westminster John Knox Press, 2011), 199.

24. Townes, "To Be Called Beloved," 198.

25. Watkins Ali, *Survival & Liberation*, 126.

26. Michael Battle, *Reconciliation: The Ubuntu Theology of Desmond Tutu*, rev. ed. (Cleveland: Pilgrim Press, 2009).
27. Mitchem, *Introducing Womanist Theology*, 46.
28. L. M. Heyns and H. J. C. Pieterse, *A Primer in Practical Theology* (Pretoria: Gnosis, 1990), 57.
29. Stephanie A. Lowery, *Identity and Ecclesiology: Their Relationship among Select African Theologians* (Eugene: Pickwick Publications, 2017), 25.

Chapter 2

Life Arenas

Faith is about life. What was it that Moses said to Israel? "I call heaven and earth to witness against you today that I have set before you life and death, blessings and curses. Choose life so that you and your descendants may live" (Deuteronomy 30:19, NRSV). Faith is indeed about life. Faith involves finding meaning and purpose and living to the fullest. It is also about finding hope amid challenging times, knowing that something greater than us is at work on earth and beyond. Moses's words to Israel are a powerful reminder that we have a choice in life. We can choose to live in a way that is life giving, or we can choose to live in a way that is destructive. Faith helps us to choose life because it gives us a vision of what life can be like when it is lived to the fullest.

In this chapter we will learn about life arenas as the multifaceted domains of our lives where we embody our beliefs, where our identity and experiences reflect the application of our faith, and where we encounter the consequences of our choices. In this chapter, we explore the various ways in which congregations play a pivotal role in individual development across different aspects of life, also known as life arenas. The chapter examines the strategies and mechanisms through which religious communities can empower their members to grow in the specific domains that matter most to them. By dissecting the intersection of faith and personal growth within life arenas, we will illustrate the positive impact congregations have on the human development of their participants.

We will also explore the dynamic designated unlimited conversation and explore how Galilee is a marker for all places we live more aligned with faith.

So, to begin, note how Craig Dykstra cautions against worshipping communities succumbing to a pattern of mutual self-destruction, that is, replacing spiritual nourishment with detrimental cultural influences. He proposes an alternative path, one where the church serves as a guiding force, fostering mutual growth among individuals as they navigate, and sometimes redeem, the intricate field of life.[1]

A congregation can effectively nurture individual growth by encouraging members to:

- recognize and name daily activities that shape their lives;
- identify and address negative influences that hinder their progress;
- embrace face-to-face conversations as a powerful tool for positive change;
- connect their everyday experiences to God's redemptive purpose through Jesus Christ; and
- by fostering these practices, empower individuals to grow spiritually and contribute to God's transformative plan for humanity.

THE REALITY OF MONDAY

Indeed, faith is about things too great for us to know. At midnight, after a long day, we are outside and see a trace of the Milky Way. We tremble. The universe speeds along with or without our knowledge. Creation holds more than we can comprehend. The psalmist is right: "I do not occupy myself with things too great and too marvelous for me" (Psalm 131).

Then, of course, there is the reality of Monday. As the Lord's Day fades into the backdrop of the week, we face the inescapability of Monday, a day where the collective experience of worship gives way to the diverse and often isolating routines of our individual lives. For a moment, imagine the experiences of Jamie. Below is Jamie's Monday as director of human resources in a small company:

- She wakes at 7:00 and listens to NPR's *Morning Edition*: a report on climate change from NASA.
- Jamie arrives at work at 9:00 ready for a 9:30 presentation on diversity, equity, and inclusion.

- Noon brings lunch with Mom and Dad, who are deciding whether to move to a smaller home.
- Back at work, Jamie hosts a Zoom meeting with other human resource leaders in the state.
- At her children's school, waiting for the bell to ring, she stands outside talking with other parents.
- She attends the church finance meeting at 7:00, and the topic is the mission budget.

Jamie spends Monday and almost every day moving from place to place, from work to family to church. What is true for Jamie is true for most of us. We move through a variety of life activities. For the Formative Program, we called the many places where one's life exists life arenas. As educators, we applied the work of Jürgen Habermas regarding lifeworlds and systems to the many spaces and behaviors we occupy every day. Initially, you may find it difficult to distinguish how our use of life arenas differs from Habermas's identification of lifeworlds. For greater clarity, we now address the way we chose to talk about the worlds in which we live, breathe, and have our being.

LIFEWORLDS AND LIFE ARENAS

Philosopher Jürgen Habermas used the term "lifeworld" to denote our reality.[2] Your lifeworld includes your family life, interactions with neighbors, volunteering at places like the men's recovery center, spending time at the county park, and much more, including participation in a congregation. The term "lifeworld," as used by Habermas, also includes the interests and connections you have with others, like the bond between jazz enthusiasts. Lifeworlds are also physical places, such as a sanctuary or a school classroom.

What represents and shapes our lifeworlds the most is conversation. It's the simple act of saying "hello" to your neighbor, calling up a friend for a chat, discussing the Psalms in Sunday school, attending a school board meeting, or talking about your upcoming vacation with a work friend while walking during a lunch break.

Habermas argues that within our lifeworlds, there are systems—concerns the Apostle Paul in Ephesians 1:21 calls "principalities and powers." Thus, he differentiates lifeworlds and systems. For Habermas, systems are activities that have become routine or institutionalized, and they can turn into forces that are destructive. Conversation within these systems can become robotic or, worse, influenced by hidden and hard-to-spot pressures. Think of how exchanges on X (formerly Twitter) or any similar platform can become mean and out of control so quickly. So it is with systems.

Within these systems, meaningful conversation has drifted into a foggy realm. Sometimes the lack of clarity is because the topic is considered too sensitive or controversial. Additionally, having a meaningful conversation within these lifeworld systems might be simply indecipherable. Think how hard it is to get a direct answer from an insurance company: "Why did my deductible change?"

Imagine a young woman who sings in the First Baptist Church choir. She's been in a terrible car accident where her mother tragically lost her life. She has been unconscious for several days. The medical staff, at the request of the family, has not told her of her mother's death. Then, while she's recovering in the intensive care unit, she stumbles upon a Facebook post from someone she doesn't know well, and that's how she finds out about her mother's death. It's a devastating and impersonal way to receive such life-altering news, even though we may think of Facebook as a personal platform.

According to Habermas, when complex systems become deeply woven into our everyday lives (lifeworlds), it can get tricky to find the right words to deal with complicated situations. This can lead to distorted communication, a loss of meaningful conversations, and even make difficult situations worse. By highlighting the notion of these impersonal systems, Habermas draws attention to the complexities inherent in our social structures. He encourages us to critically examine the systems that shape our lifeworlds, identifying those that hinder human flourishing.

To nurture our personal growth and fulfill God's purpose, we can change how we interact with the lifeworlds we inhabit. By recognizing that our presence and interactions may vary in different contexts and by seeking to appreciate others in those settings, we then create a foundation for meaningful conversations. These genuine conversations strengthen our connections and promote healthier exchanges, ultimately contributing to our growth as individuals.[3]

Now, let's shift our focus to distinguishing between lifeworlds and what we refer to as life arenas.

LIFE ARENAS

In the Formative Program, we used the term "life arena" to encapsulate both Habermas's concept of lifeworlds and the impact of systems.[4] We wanted to merge the concepts of lifeworlds and systems to emphasize that congregations can be places where people grow positively or places that dishonor the unique experiences of others.

Congregations exhibit positive formative power when the community ethos provides immunity from empty or confusing conversations. Congregations can and should be the growing space for people to be safe from inane conversation, a safe haven from the Tower of Babel (Genesis 11:1–9).

The concept of life arena encompasses the complex aspects of human life, acknowledging that various factors such as culture, ethnicity, gender, socioeconomic status, personal history, and especially participation in a congregation influence our development. When we refer to life arenas, we acknowledge that each arena carries a distinct combination of beliefs, identity, and actions, each representing a system that exists on a spectrum of sin and redemption.

Below we introduce a variety of life arenas, some referenced in the introduction:

- family
- vocation
- finances
- wellness
- the arts
- education
- social justice
- being a neighbor
- care for the ill
- charity
- creation care
- mental health

- parenting
- specific hobbies
- teaching

DIFFERENT SELVES

How we show up, our way of being, and how we speak, act, and feel may differ from person to person and from situation to situation. The difference is shaped by many factors, including who we are in terms of our human development and who and what has had a profound effect on our behavior, feelings, and thinking. We show up differently depending on the arena we are in; arenas shape our inner world and how we inhabit external vistas. Consistent with womanist theology, human beings are not meant to be standardized or molded to fit a particular blueprint. We are inherently multifaceted, a multiplicity of selves playing with a plurality of ways to show up on life's various stages.

Consider a pastor who displays different behaviors, speech patterns, and emotional responses when coaching her daughter's basketball team compared to when offering a benediction at the end of a worship service. In the coaching arena, she may adopt a more assertive and directive communication style, exhibit competitive actions, and internally experience a sense of excitement or urgency. Conversely, while leading Sunday worship, she may speak with reverence and deliver a benediction evoking emotions of gratitude and hope among parishioners.

We shape the places we inhabit, and such places shape us.

People must make sense of many different selves in different life arenas at any given time. As the arenas we navigate multiply, we must adapt, become more fluid, and develop in new ways.

Professor of biblical studies Mary Ann Tolbert writes:

> My sense of self of who I am shifts over time and varies in different contexts (for example, daughter to my parents, teacher to my students, woman in a group of men, white in a group of people of color, and so on) with each different subjective "identity" position requiring distinctive behavior, language usage, dress, and so on.[5]

A first-year high school student named Kevin describes his experience at a new school during sharing time at youth group:

All of a sudden, you are in a new school with new friends. The year before, people knew your name and knew what you were about; then you find yourself in a new place with new people, new expectations, and new things to do. It's like being on a train platform with the train leaving the station. If you don't get on really quick, you are going to be left behind. Then, to make matters even more complicated, sometimes all these new and old groups collide with each other, and it's like everything is ricocheting off the wall. It's easy to feel lost.[6]

Our sense of self undergoes transformation and evolves as we navigate through various life arenas. Robert Kegan uses the phrase "in over our heads"[7] as we find ourselves in situations where the complexity of an arena surpasses our current level of capabilities. It is crucial to note that when individuals like Kevin encounter challenges in certain arenas, such as school, it does not necessarily indicate personal inadequacy. Instead, challenges emerge when the complexities and demands of a particular arena, or a confluence of arenas, exceed prior experiences. This necessitates adaptation and growth to navigate these new complexities.

BEING SEEN

A clear habit in life arenas is encountering other human beings. Whether it's in the realm of work or at the church small group we attend, we come across one another. This interaction often takes the form of direct encounters or, as philosopher Emmanuel Levinas refers to them in his work *Ethics and Infinity*, face-to-face occasions.[8] Levinas does not mean exclusively literal face-to face interactions, though such interactions might in fact be so. Rather, these interactions involve positive human sociality, appropriate intimacy, and ethical responsibility.

Nowadays, we might use the phrase "I was seen" as the recognition of being truly acknowledged and recognized as a unique person in the midst of the larger social design. A marker of vibrant congregations is that they are a home where face-to-face interactions thrive. These in-person encounters are a formative practice field for fostering connection and understanding beyond the church walls.

A pastor describes the Ash Wednesday imposition of ashes:

I look everyone in the eye, the mother holding her infant, the man just diagnosed with lung cancer, the teenager who just learned she was not alone, others that can barely drag themselves out of bed to school, or the grandfather delighted that his grandson was just elected to the school board. I don't know the words to say how powerful this is. I used to hide that I was crying when I said, "Dust you are"—like to the baby. Now I don't mind them seeing my tears.

We believe life arenas, particularly the congregation, can be places of grace where we can be seen and we can see others more clearly. What are the words attributed to Paul? "For now we see in a mirror, dimly, but then we will see face to face. Now I know only in part; then I will know fully, even as I have been fully known" (1 Corinthians 13:12).

As a pastor, I (Tim) recall a Bible study where a participant revealed that he had been convicted of a crime and served almost three years in prison.

> Silence.
> Then another member said, "That must have been so hard for you."
> The participant responded, "You mean it is okay that I said that here?"

Being seen means more than just being noticed. Yes, the phrase "being seen" may be a colloquial way of mirroring what Levinas meant by face-to-face encounters. Both designations represent feeling understood and validated for your thoughts and experiences. It's comforting to know that someone is genuinely listening and trying to connect with the real you. This creates a sense of belonging, where you feel that your voice matters and your perspective is valued. It empowers you to be authentic, knowing that you will be accepted, not judged. When I experience this at a church, I know I'm in a congregation where I (Tim) want to participate.

We've examined what we mean by life arenas, acting differently in any number of them, and the importance of being seen. Let's now turn to the idea, actually the reality, of unlimited conversation.

UNLIMITED CONVERSATION

Let's consider the role of conversation and sacred texts in reinforcing face-to-face relationships within life arenas. Recall that the opening to the Gospel of Mark begins with "The beginning of the good news of Jesus Christ" (Mark 1:1). This is an intentional rhetorical device to start the Gospel. If it was first a verbal, even conversational rendering to the Markan community, then the first verse functions as "Once upon a time." The first verse might be a purposeful reference to "In the beginning" in Genesis 1. The opening to which Mark refers might also be the entire Gospel movement, the lived experience of Jesus Christ in people's lives.[9]

We add still another possibility. The Gospel is perpetually in a moment of inception. Creation holds the potential for perpetual renewal. Therefore, the Gospel resembles an ongoing conversation that never concludes, as it continuously begins and begins anew.

Therefore, the Gospel of Mark is a living conversation, constantly being renewed and redefined as it is shared among the faithful. The Good News of Jesus Christ is like a never-ending story, always starting over as it is passed on from one person to another.

Imagine that you are meeting a good friend for lunch whom you haven't seen for five years, perhaps someone you went to school with. Have you noticed that often you feel as if it hasn't been a five-year absence? You pick up where you left off. It is as if, all of a sudden, the relationship hadn't been put on pause.

Religious beginnings repeat repeatedly. Life in Christ does not produce the commodity of a neat and tidy end. Carrying faith into life arenas is not confined to linear, chronological time but encompasses a deeper dimension known as kairos time. Kairos time refers to the opportune moment, the right time, or the appointed time in which God's activity intersects with our lives. It transcends the constraints of beginnings and endings and invites us into a heightened awareness of God's work in the present moment.

Now, let's look at the ending of the Gospel of Mark. Mark 16 describes the resurrection of Jesus Christ. The specific settings described in Mark 16 include the empty tomb where Jesus's body was placed after his crucifixion. The account includes an angel who informs the women about God raising Jesus.

During this section of the Gospel of Mark, the events unfold in and around Jerusalem, which serves as the pivotal setting—the life arena—for this part of the narrative.

Mark 16 includes two endings of the Gospel. The original, shorter ending of Mark's Gospel ends with verse 8 and is open-ended. Verse 8 ends mid-sentence with enigmatic words: "They told no one nothing, afraid they were for." The Greek ends mid-sentence with a preposition.

What did these words mean? Did the women tell anyone that Christ was raised? And if they did not, as the witness suggests, how did others hear the news? Wouldn't others who listened to the Markan witness wonder how they came to hear if no one spoke because of fear? I mean, if literally no one said anything, how did we come to hear of the empty tomb? Precisely what were the terms of this proclamation that ends in mid-sentence? What kind of nonconclusive scenario is this?

Mark's introduction and abbreviated ending captures the essence of our multifaceted lives. Our experiences and conversations in different areas of life are like ongoing entry points, not a single linear path. Our projects and commitments are ongoing journeys, not a dead end. Mark tells his Gospel with an abbreviated ending so listeners sense they are part of the "to be continued" project called Jesus Christ. Mark ends the Gospel in mid-sentence because there is no ending to Christ's ministry. The "ending," or more accurately, the continuation of Christ's ministry, is our life. The Gospel of Mark is a book without an ending. Our development is a never-ending story.

Many parts of Scripture, particularly parables, were meant to start conversations rather than give straightforward lessons. Think of large portions of all four Gospels as open-ended stories, encouraging first-century listeners to discuss their meanings.[10] Jesus tells a story about a wayward younger son, a diligent older son, and an extraordinarily loving father. Instead of Jesus wrapping it up neatly as depicted in the Gospels, Jesus invites discussion. The crowd comes forward with various interpretations. As the story gets retold, new insights emerge with each telling. This cycle of multiple meanings continues until the parable reaches us today. And even then, there's still more to unpack and consider. Think about this. It isn't an unusual assertion. Haven't we heard someone say in Sunday school, "I learn something new every time we study this Bible passage"?

Instead of handing out straightforward answers or moral lessons, parables encouraged people to get involved with the stories and relate them to their own lives. This hands-on way of teaching matches the overall goal of Scripture, which isn't just to give facts but to transform lives by getting people actively involved with its teachings.

Such is the gospel of unlimited conversation.

When we think of Scripture as a conversation rather than a set-in-stone text, we become active players in applying the words, letting them speak to our own situations and guide us toward personal development. Perhaps this is why Gil Rendle, church leadership consultant, says, "Conversation is the currency of change."[11]

Conversations serve as words and actions when we occupy a particular life arena. Let's say the conversation is about something as ordinary as, say, baking a pie. Conversation serves various purposes. If the pie making involves a grandmother teaching a grandson, conversation can be instructional, a series of "how-to" steps. Conversation also marks a personal interaction, expression of feelings, building connections, and so forth.

On to the next conversation. Let's overhear a conversation about something as significant as a visit to Cincinnati's National Underground Railroad Freedom Center. Picture two individuals engaged in discussion as they make their way out of the Freedom Center.

One person says, "That was very uncomfortable because I know my ancestors enslaved people."

The other person observes, "Now you know exactly why we needed to make this trip." From this beginning, the two people talk about their experience at the Freedom Center on the one-hundred-mile trip home. Through conversation, we put ourselves in others' shoes, work together, and sort out disagreements without getting out of hand. As the two people drive home, they become more aware of what matters most to one another. They become aware of their different life experiences and understand the different points of view they hold. Talking with others involves feelings, building connections, and learning. Thus, conversation within life arenas can enhance our growth in trail markers, such as self-differentiation, emotional regulation, and attachment. Since conversations never genuinely end, there is always more to say about almost everything, from the mundane to the sacred.

Note the multitude of conversations that take place in congregational life:

- dialogue at Bible studies
- consensus building at committee meetings
- pastoral conversations
- informal conversations at fellowship events
- sharing in small groups
- guest presenters followed by questions (and answers)
- talk with strangers met during a mission trip
- prayer groups
- the sermon as a possibility for conversation[12]

So, keep talking, keep listening, keep conversing. You will grow as a person. And know that you can continue or revisit every conversation. Every conversation you have continues previous dialogues, even if you are not conscious of it being so. To paraphrase Gil Rendle, "conversation is the currency of life arenas."

Now, the power of conversation for growth leads us back to the Gospel of Mark, back to "to be continued" conversations, and ultimately to a life arena called Galilee.

GALILEE

In Mark 16, a young man dressed in a white robe tells Mary Magdalene, Mary the mother of James, and Salome, not to be afraid (they were afraid, very afraid) because Jesus has gone ahead into Galilee. The young man instructs the three to go to Galilee.

Galilee, beyond being a geographical location, holds symbolic importance. It is the life arena where Jesus carried out his mission of preaching, teaching, and healing. Galilee became the stage for transformative encounters, where Jesus blessed people, challenged societal norms, and proclaimed the kingdom of God. It was in Galilee that Jesus called his disciples, performed miracles, and spun parables as an invitation to ongoing consideration of God's realm. The totality of the life arenas in which followers of Christ participate is Galilee.

Expanding upon this biblical narrative, we can understand Galilee as a metaphor for the broader scope of the disciples' participation in the mission of Christ. Galilee represents the territories, the life arenas where followers of Jesus are called to proclaim and embody the Good News. Recognizing Galilee as our collective life arena invites us to consider the significance of our (individual) life arenas, where we can be agents of transformation and bearers of the Gospel. It encourages us to see every encounter, every conversation, and every act of service as part of our participation in the ongoing ministry of Christ.

As David Buttrick preached in a sermon at Duke University, "our territory is world."[13]

ULTIMATE CONCERNS

Years ago, in dusty New York classrooms, the theologian Paul Tillich spoke of God differently than his colleagues (Reinhold Niebuhr, for example). I invite you to turn on your imagination. Tillich's lips hold a cigarette off to the side, he speaks with whatever is beyond a German accent, and he wears slacks he has worn for three days. If you were there, you'd take notes like:

- God is Itself.
- God is the ground of being.
- Ultimate concerns may be symbols for God.
- What matters most to you? There you will find Being itself.

Congregants we worked with during our Formative Power of Your Congregation project may not have heard of Tillich, except perhaps participants from near New Harmony, Indiana, where his remains rest. However, one's commitment to an ultimate concern requires both thinking about the concern and participation in the concern.

Tillich writes, "Faith as ultimate concern is an act of the total personality. It happen[s] in the center of the personal life and includes all its elements."[14]

A young man puts a "no weapons allowed" sticker on the school's front door. He's concerned for his safety and for the safety of his classmates. Two days later the sticker disappears. He has a rebellious streak, so the next day, with determination, he once again places a "no weapons allowed" sticker on the door until it stays. This goes back and forth for several days. At one point, the sticker stays for an entire school week.

Ask him why the sticker, and he says, "My brother lives in Australia. They don't have guns and they don't have school shootings."

The life arena is the school, and the ultimate concern is specifically safety and weapons-free classrooms. These priorities are significant to him, and he acts consistently with his convictions. His determination shows that he has a rooted sense of purpose.

What is the relationship between life arenas and ultimate concerns? Life arenas are the different areas of our lives, such as work, family, relationships, and hobbies. Our ultimate concern is the thing that gives our lives meaning and purpose. It can influence all aspects of our lives, including our beliefs, identities, and activities in each life arena.

For example, if our ultimate concern is social justice, we may choose to work in a nonprofit organization or volunteer our time to a cause we believe in. We may also choose to raise our children with a sense of social responsibility.

If our ultimate concern is creativity, we may choose to pursue a career in the arts or spend our free time writing, painting, or making music. We may also surround ourselves with people who inspire us creatively.

Our ultimate concern can also help us to navigate difficult choices. For example, if our ultimate concern is family, we may be more likely to choose a job that allows us to spend time with our loved ones, even if it means sacrificing some income or career advancement opportunities.

Furthermore, our ultimate concern makes us unique as individuals and gives our lives meaning. It is important to reflect on what our ultimate concern is and to develop an identity that supports not only the ultimate concern but our participation in that concern. An essential form this reflection takes is conversation (see the discussion above). Words connect to action. Action begets learning. Learning and developing, if we so choose, occur throughout our life span.

All of us have things that matter a lot to us, places and activities we deeply care about. But here's the catch: sometimes these things we care about so much can actually be harmful. It could be something as serious as supporting a cause or a movement that ends up hurting a lot of people, even though we might not realize it at first. Or, in less obvious ways, it can involve being overly focused on a particular area of life while neglecting our responsibilities or relationships over time, which can cause lasting emotional and physical pain for ourselves and others. It's like we're so focused on what we think is important that we don't see the damage it might be causing.

Yet we can choose that which is life giving and modulate how we pay attention to that which matters most to us. The author James K. A. Smith says, "You are what you want."[15]

Smith contends that when we attend to our desires faithfully, they guide us toward beneficial actions. Our desires serve a purpose, aiming to propel us toward a more enriching and satisfying life

Yet, don't forget, desires influence our subconscious and shape our actions before we even have time to rationalize them. Intense desires can become compulsions that override clear thinking and self-control. When we become consumed by a desire, it can be challenging to resist acting on it, even if the behavior is harmful.

At the church I served in Xenia, Ohio, we hosted four twelve-step groups during the week. I had to watch my pride because we were the only church in town with twelve-step meetings. Many participants had, often understandably, given in to the desire to misuse alcohol. A yearning for peace, turned into harmful desire, developed into a damaging ultimate concern. However, participating in a community, engaging in ongoing conversations, often testimony, led to personal growth and character development.

Twelve-step participants better understand themselves, their motivations, and their behavior. People attend to managing their feelings, building solid relationships, and understanding how both good and bad experiences shape them. Even if they don't use fancy words and phrases (secure attachment) to describe what is happening, such dynamics are fundamental for ongoing growth.

Let's return to the writing of James K. A. Smith. What he found among people who are being shaped by their experiences and beliefs is that they have certain things in life that matter deeply to them. Many of them didn't initially connect these deep concerns with their religious or congregational life, but they did find elements of life that were worth dedicating their whole selves to.

We invite you to consider comments made by Formative Power participants:

When I was in high school, I played on the basketball team. The coach meant the world to me. My uniforms are now stitched together as a blanket. And maybe this is why I like teaching and coaching.

I love music, every kind of music. I am from El Salvador, and my favorite music is heavy metal, Metallica, and such. I live for that time of day when I can sit down and listen to that music play.

Why do we settle for such manufactured food? I don't want to in any way. That's why I plant my garden every March and harvest every September.

I have walked in many protests in Indianapolis. I'm a Black man, and I'm a target. My goal is not to just walk but to talk, to make sure people listen to what I say.

These comments express significant value to the speakers, reflecting their ultimate concerns. The Formative Power of Your Congregations' proposition suggests that when our deepest concerns are intertwined with congregational practices, our life experiences become more profound, and our expertise in these ultimate matters contributes to a well-lived life.

All of us are embarked on a journey; it is inevitable. Framed by faith in a redeeming God, our journey can be seen as the development of all the trail markers (such as authority or competence) at one episode or another.

Some journeys are outward focused, where congregations aim to cultivate their participants' growth in areas such as caring for creation, combating racism, addressing food scarcity, and performing acts of charity. Other congregations encourage their members to explore their inner live (yes, think of our interior lives as Galilee).

Cultivated by the Beatitudes (the pastor says that's his scripture), a church from Ohio embarked on a brave mission: to relocate to one of Indiana's most impoverished zip codes. Led by their pastor, these mostly first-generation immigrant congregants uprooted their lives again (they actually moved their households) to immerse themselves in a community facing significant challenges such as access to food and health care.

Their vision? To become more than neighbors—they wanted to be testaments of compassion, actively redeeming this life arena through acts of blessing.

The move was unusual but not a strange or dubious undertaking. The congregation was moving to a community that also included first-generation immigrants from their homeland. The mission wasn't about a grand vision. Their life arena was the everyday, the small moments of connection forged at mailboxes, shared laughter at church-sponsored street festivals, the quiet support offered sitting on a bench on a spring evening. It was about building trust, understanding the challenges their new community faced, and learning to listen to stories (often the same ones repeatedly) with open hearts and open minds.

The boundary between evangelism and simple kindness expanded so that prayer, play, friendship, and connection all existed as a contextual ecclesiology, though folks might have called it just plain church.

One leader within this congregation articulated their vision. Soon after their move, when people heard of the church, the response would be, "Oh, you are the church in *that* zip code." The not-so-subtle slight did not stop the congregants. They aspired to be known as "the church that makes friends."

To an outsider, the activities may have appeared as any number of neighborhood occasions. After all, providing stuffed animal prizes for the Frisbee-throwing contest is not an activity highlighted in a twenty-first-century systematic theology framework. However, the work of this wonderfully idiosyncratic congregation represents the values of womanist theology (again, even if they would never use that phrase), which emphasizes the feminist values of relationships and face-to-face encounters. This itinerant church didn't need fancy theological jargon to express their mission; it lived in the shared smiles at a taco truck, listening to the stories of people who a year ago had lived in another country, and the promise "I'll pray for you" after that springtime conversation on a park bench.

Imagine life takes place in a never-ending field. Home is to the east, work's the hustle zone to the west, and inside your head? That's a whole other wild show where our interior lives confound, where we chase dreams and wrestle with desires. Yet this field extends even more. Your neighborhood, with houses, schools (minus the weapons!), stores, and scary places you are reluctant to tell others about—this is all part of your home turf. This planet Earth, with its blue beauty and life-or-death challenges, is a vast space to explore. All this is our home, our own personal Galilee, always there, waiting to be seen; the arenas of our lives where we grow ever more human, redeemed by grace forever.

FORMATIVE ASSETS

Several years ago, the basketball player Bill Bradley (later a U.S. senator) was the subject of a book titled *A Sense of Where You Are*.[16]

When you participate in a congregation, you develop a sense of where you are. The sense of where you are informs who you are.

You may be at work. You may be at home. You may be on the street. You may be in front of a tablet screen. You may be in the middle of a conversation. You may know exactly where you are because you are home. You may be praying with the small church group in which you participate. In any one of these areas, you may have developed a sense of where you are, what matters most to you, and what forms your ultimate concern.

The diversity of life situations is infinite. Anything can happen. You may be walking through the doors on your way to your first day on the job, being greeted by someone who is in the twelve-step group at your church. You know not to say anything so as not to break confidentiality. You may find yourself in a job that pays more than you ever dreamed. You might turn down the dream job because it would take you away from your volunteer time at the women's shelter. You could be the man hearing the testimony of a women's shelter resident and realize you have nothing helpful to say; listening is the way.

Your life matters. What matters the most to you? What life arenas wait for you?

Have you read these words from Dietrich Bonhoeffer?

> I discovered later, and I'm still discovering right up to this moment, that it is only by living completely in this world that one learns to have faith. By this-worldliness, I mean living unreservedly in life's duties, problems, successes, and failures. In so doing, we throw ourselves completely into the arms of God, taking seriously not our own sufferings but those of God in the world. That, I think, is faith.[17]

QUESTIONS FOR REFLECTION

1. What matters most to you? What are your ultimate concerns?
2. Who do you talk with about your ultimate concerns?
3. In what ways is the conversation ongoing?

NOTES

1. Craig Dykstra, *Growing in the Life of Faith: Education and Christian Practices* (Louisville: Westminster John Knox Press, 1999).
2. Jürgen Habermas, *The Theory of Communicative Action*, vol. 2, *Lifeworld and System: A Critique of Functionalist Reason*, trans. Thomas McCarthy (Boston: Beacon Press, 1987).
3. Gordon Finlayson, *Habermas: A Very Short Introduction* (New York: Oxford University Press, 2005).
4. Finlayson, *Habermas*.
5. Fernando F. Segovia and Mary Ann Tolbert, eds., *Reading from this Place*, vol. 1, *Social Location and Biblical Interpretation in the United States* (Minneapolis: Augsburg Fortress, 1995), 310.
6. Quote from a sermon roundtable at Westminster Presbyterian Church in Xenia, Ohio, on October 15, 2000. See also John S. McClure, *The Roundtable Pulpit: Where Leadership and Preaching Meet* (Nashville: Abingdon Press, 1995).
7. Robert Kegan, *In Over Our Heads: The Mental Demands of Modern Life* (Cambridge, MA: Harvard University Press, 1994).
8. Emmanuel Levinas, *Ethics and Infinity: Conversations with Philippe Nemo*, trans. Richard A. Cohen (Pittsburgh: Duquesne University Press, 1985).
9. Aspects of the interpretation of Mark's Gospel come from a 2014 conversation with the Rev. William Steele.
10. John Dominic Crossan, *The Power of Parable: How Fiction by Jesus Became Fiction about Jesus* (New York: HarperCollins, 2012).
11. Gil Rendle, "Leadership Means 'Pushing People to Purpose,'" *Faith & Leadership*, May 31, 2016, https://faithandleadership.com/gil-rendle-leadership-means-pushing-people-purpose (accessed October 24, 2023).
12. McClure, *Roundtable Pulpit*.
13. David Buttrick, *Speaking Conflict: Stories of a Controversial Jesus* (Louisville: Westminster John Knox Press, 2007), 131.
14. Paul Tillich, *Dynamics of Faith* (New York: HarperCollins, 1957), 4.
15. James K. A. Smith, *You Are What You Love* (Grand Rapids, MI: Brazos Press, 2016).

16. John McPhee, *A Sense of Where You Are: Bill Bradley at Princeton* (New York: Farrar, Straus & Giroux, 1999).

17. Dietrich Bonhoeffer, *Letters and Papers from Prison*, Dietrich Bonhoeffer Works 8 (Minneapolis: Fortress Press, 2010), 486.

Chapter 3

Congregational Practices

When congregations gather, some do so in large steeple structures, others in living rooms, and still others in storefront spaces. Some come dressed in their "Sunday best" while others are in casual attire. Some sit in old wooden pews, others in folding chairs. Regardless of where or how we congregate, we come together as people of faith to nourish our souls, deepen our faith, be reminded of who God is, and find ways old and new to retell the stories of our faith that shape the identity, beliefs, and activity of our congregation. We accomplish all of this through congregational practices.

In chapter 1, we explored our theology of congregational life that informs a congregation's beliefs, identity, and activity. In chapter 2, we established how faith was about life and the areas of life that matter most to people. This chapter will examine congregational practices and their impact on individuals. Human development occurs in various settings beyond congregations, such as schools, families, or community organizations. However, congregations offer a distinctive role in supporting human development. This unique role is due to the religious nature of congregations and the activities congregants engage in to express values such as faith, hope, and love.

To start, we will establish a definition of congregational practices, naming the primary actions and rituals that occur within religious assemblies. These practices serve as a framework that shapes the way of life for individuals involved, even if they are not explicitly prescribed. By actively participating in these practices, individuals become immersed in a faith-infused way of life that molds their beliefs, values, and behaviors. These practices inform congregants' lives, every day, not just on the day of worship. These practices, over time, contribute to the development of human beings regarding key markers such as openness to transcendence, taking initiative, owning one's authority, and more.

In addition to exploring the positive aspects of congregational practices, we will confront the reality that congregations can wield destructive power over their adherents. Despite their potential for growth and positive influence, congregations are not immune to harmful dynamics or negative outcomes. We will critically examine these detrimental aspects and their impact on individuals within congregational settings.

By addressing both the positive and negative dimensions of congregational influence, this chapter seeks to present a balanced and nuanced understanding of the formative power that congregations hold.

DEFINING CONGREGATIONAL PRACTICES

Congregational practices refer to contextualized activities commonly observed in churches, including preaching, teaching, and caring for souls. These practices aim to align individuals with their religious beliefs and commitments, serving God's purposes for the world. Within Christian traditions, congregational practices can be understood as patterns of communal action that create openings in our lives where the grace, mercy, and presence of God may be made known to us.[1] They are places where the mystery of God is experienced and, in the end, these are not ultimately our practices but forms of participation in the practice of God.[2] When we participate in congregational practices, the whole of life is engaged because we who practice them are whole selves that do not and cannot check life at the front door of the church.

Even within the same denomination, congregations located just a mile apart may have different forms of the same ritual. For example, one congregation might practice baptism by immersion in a sanctuary pool, while another may prefer immersion in a nearby lake. Furthermore, within a single assembly, a range of practices can relate to the same activity. Consider a congregation with two preachers. One pastor delivers extemporaneous sermons, directly applying a Bible passage to various life situations. This preacher may illustrate the parable of the prodigal son with a series of stories that illustrate unconditional love. Alternatively, the other clergyperson may follow an expository style, starting from Genesis 1:1 and interpreting each verse through Genesis

1:12, concluding the sermon with a message about how the struggle between good and evil is a part of our daily lives, just like it was in the story of Eden. In these examples, both sermons demonstrate how congregations use preaching to connect biblical teachings with everyday life, although in contrasting ways.

Elements of worship in a congregation, such as a sermon, reflect Christian practices within the sanctuary and inspire and shape the congregants' actions and testimonies in their everyday lives, in the various life arenas where participants live and have their being. The description above of congregational practices, particularly the sermon, is from a practical theology point of view. Sociologists also define what a congregation is. Sociologist Mark Chaves writes that a congregation is a social institution in which activities tend to be commonplace among people, some religious specialists and others not. The emphasis is on the relationship between people and the sociological elements held mainly in common.[3]

Theological views of a congregation do not have to be in an oppositional relationship with a sociological view. This is why we have used the phrase "practical ecclesiology" (see chapter 1) to describe how churches, powered by congregational practices, can actively engage with their communities and the world around them. It's about understanding the beliefs, identity, and practices of a church and using that understanding to make a positive impact on society.

To illustrate this, imagine a college student who returns home for Thanksgiving and attends worship at the church where he was baptized. The sermon is based on Matthew 8, where Jesus emphasizes the importance of recognizing him in the presence of the least among us. Later, back at school, the student attends sociology class, where the professor discusses the social forces that perpetuate the inequitable distribution of resources, highlighting the forces that keep wealth in particular families as it is passed down through generations. In response, the student contributes to the discussion by saying, "Okay, so wealth tends to be held within certain families over time, it doesn't mean we can't challenge the way money is held on to." The student recognized a connection between the message of the sermon and the lessons in their sociology class. The sermon showed a more person-to-person teaching. The sociology class leaned into systems. The student realized that both were speaking to the importance of challenging inequality and working toward justice, even when such efforts seemed daunting. They saw that faith and a sociological point of view were not in opposition but rather complementary forces for change.

MUSICAL CONGREGATIONAL PRACTICES AND IDENTITY

Congregational practices involving music are particularly powerful conduits of formation throughout life, but especially in early life. Neuropsychology research confirms that the brain's memory systems are at their most efficient during childhood and early adulthood. A key reason that we often return to music from this period of our lives is that it reminds us of who we are, as it is during these formative years that we establish the beliefs that form our identity.[4]

Congregational practices involving music that shapes who we are can be understood neurologically, but they can also be understood sociohistorically.

As a child, I (Christina) vividly remember the musical expressions of my congregation, from singing and dancing to instruments playing familiar hymns. For instance, there was this one song that preceded the moment in service when our congregation could greet one another with a hug or handshake. Many times, with what as a child I could discern as the worship leader's subtle frustration, the congregation had to be prompted several times to return to our seats and resume the service. The refrain began with the words "I love you with the love of the Lord," repeated a few times over, and eventually only the instrumental persisted. This instrumental was the soundtrack to not only greeting each other but asking how the other was doing and being updated on life. We would check in with "Hey! How's your son doing?" or "You ever find that new vehicle you were in the market for because I may know someone looking to sell," or "How did your hospital procedure go?" or simply looking eye-to-eye, delighting in the other with the words "It's good to see you!" These activities, enacted every Sunday, shaped the way we saw ourselves as connected to a community who cared about one another.

The connection was not limited to the moments of singing the same lyrics; the connection was a concern about life. This practice of concern about the lives of others, I believe, followed me and others into the concern for neighbors and community members and entire communities—bringing "to life," as it were, the lyrics describing the love of God that we sang of as a congregation each week.

Music and identity formation is evident intergenerationally as well. In the case of Black communities, music expressed through song by our ancestors was a bridge between the harsh realities of day-to-day life and the ability to transcend beyond this material world. Songs like "Swing Low, Sweet Chariot" were ways of accessing the presence of the Divine "withness" of God amid the toil and evil that was enslavement. This and other songs like it were also subversive and were used as a way for enslaved Africans to communicate information undetected. Singing and drumming enacted through call and response facilitated connection to ancestral identities rooted in a land of diverse tribes and enabled identity retention. From the invisible institution of the Black Church to the present day, music continues to serve as a portal to African religious practices, beliefs, traditions, and identity. The same is true for many cultures and peoples. Music is inherently bound up with personal and collective identity and can recall self-defining experiences with potency.[5]

Given the cultural identity implications of music, it is no wonder that as a congregational practice, music has the power to form us. Moreover, a theology of worship through music affirms that song is rich with meaningful texts that speak to who God is to us, and what we believe. In the same way that music shapes, affirms, and teaches us in formative ways, so does prayer, Christian education, preaching, the sacraments, and a whole host of contextually located practices that are unique to your congregation.

Perhaps there is the practice of hospitality, service, or visitation. Perhaps there are practices related to worship such as dancing, clapping, or shouting. It all points to creating the contours of a life together that shape who we are.

LIFE TOGETHER

A church influences our identity, beliefs, and actions. This influence goes beyond what the congregation officially says in its mission statement. It means that by being actively involved in the congregation's activities, a person grows and develops their character, however imperfect, persuaded in part by what the congregation does in practice, not just what it says on paper.

As a result, being a member of the congregation takes on a more meaningful significance. A lot is at stake. It's not just about having your name on a list; it's about the ongoing process of personal growth and development that happens as you participate in the congregation's activities. It's about how your character is shaped by experiences within the congregation.

Some new congregations, including growing congregations, forego the category of membership or call belonging by another name. The Center for Congregations knows one congregation that calls its members "co-conspirators." Perhaps the word "membership" has lost its power of attraction.

This does not mean, however, that human beings do not have a need for belonging. All but the most reclusive people belong to something—their family, a workplace, a neighborhood, a social club, and, for about 45 percent of Americans, a congregation. As Wendell Berry writes in the voice of Burley Coulter, "The way we are, we are members of each other. All of us. Everything. The difference ain't in who is a member and who is not, but in who knows it and who don't."[6]

Such participation provides people with a sense of belonging that transcends oneself, that connects one's soul with a larger purpose.

In this sense, membership in a congregation can and should be more than an inventory of requirements, say, worship attendance, pledging, or hosting the fellowship hour at least once a year. These requirements have their place. Yet the conditions of religious claims and commitments call for more. Such conditions call for membership as an experience that points to an expansive horizon beyond one's own vision. In this way, the meaning of membership can be reframed from being about the labor of volunteers who support an institution to belonging to a community that forms you and me consistent with espoused claims and commitments.

A pastor calls the Center for Congregations' office. She is asking about whether or not we make grants related to spiritual formation programs. The answer is yes, we do. When our staff person says, "Tell me more," the pastor responds by saying, "I want our congregation to build better people."

The conversation moves along. "What do you mean 'build better people'?"

The pastor says, "We have guidelines about how to become a member. But these guidelines don't really say anything about the person. I'm interested in whether or not our congregation produces people who are willing to stand up for the left out, or pray for justice (I mean really pray), or commit to sharing their faith with others. That's building better people."

In other words, the pastor wants her people to live consistent with the faith claims expressed in sermons, sacraments, prayer, and many other congregational practices.

A clergyperson, along with the church council, enthusiastically started a new congregational practice within their congregation that effectively underscores the significance of being an active member of a religious community. They introduced a booklet titled "Rule of Life," thoughtfully created, which serves as a comprehensive guidebook outlining the congregation's core values and practices.

The leader's primary objective is to inspire individuals to wholeheartedly embrace a specific way of life, a way demonstrating the faith and values of the congregation. The guidebook includes a dedicated catechism, written by an intergenerational group of members, providing answers to be learned and recited, enabling congregants to internalize their faith. Furthermore, it presents detailed descriptions of specific practices for members to engage in, one of which is the communal recitation of Psalm 23 every day at noon, where everyone pauses their activities, wherever they are, and prays the Psalm.

By consistently actively engaging with Psalm 23 at the same time each day, individuals create conditions for this text to become an integral part of their identity. This intentional and collective engagement with the Psalm enhances the likelihood that, for example, the trail markers (see chapter 4) of attachment and emotional regulation will grow.

One of the Formative Power participants shared a story about how a conversation with a stranger in the fellowship hall after worship helped him to cope with the recent death of his grandmother. While the young man was waiting in line for donuts, he found himself next to an adult whose wife had died earlier that year. The two began to talk about their losses. The young man was surprised to find that he felt a sense of comfort with this person he really didn't know. He said, "I didn't expect to have that conversation anywhere. I now know that such conversations are allowed. And they can happen at church." This anecdote illustrates the power of congregational experiences to shape our lives in profound ways. They can provide us with a sense of community, comfort, and courage. They can also teach us important lessons about life, faith, and death—what it means to be human.

Many elements make you the person you are. You are shaped by your race, your geographical location, and your genetic structure. Your personality is formed by your family, your friends, and the choices you make along the way. Education, social affiliations, and friendships influence you.

All of us are formed by the company we keep. The company we keep includes the congregation you attend. Whether you know it or not, your congregation's activities create specific thoughts, feelings, and behaviors that make you who you are. In this way, your congregation has formative power.

DIETRICH BONHOEFFER

To further explore the concept of formative experiences, let's examine the life of German theologian Dietrich Bonhoeffer, whose quote concluded the previous chapter. Bonhoeffer holds a significant influence on my (Tim) theological understanding. While my most influential theologians are the individuals I encounter in my daily life—family, friends, colleagues, and mentors—among academically trained theologians, Bonhoeffer's work resonates with me the most. Therefore, some of this section is written in the first person.

Contradictions abound in his life's story. I find God in these contradictions. For example, Bonhoeffer was a pacifist who believed Christians should not participate in violence. However, he also thought resisting evil was necessary, even if that meant using violence. He ultimately participated in a plot to assassinate Hitler, which led to Bonhoeffer's execution. Bonhoeffer believed in the importance of individual conscience and responsibility. However, he also thought Christians should live in a community with one another.

Furthermore, Bonhoeffer believed that no one could avoid feeling guilty. Trying to be perfect and avoiding conflicts is not possible; such sanctification is beyond our reach. We should be ready to help others, even if it means facing challenging situations and feeling guilty later.[7]

He also said that if we don't accept guilt for the sake of others, it goes against what Christ and Christianity represent. Bonhoeffer argued that refusing guilt when it's for a good cause contradicts our responsibility in the real world.[8]

Contradictions, rather than obstacles, can represent openness to broader perspectives. When I loosen my grip on rigid stances of "right" and "wrong," I open myself to explore diverse viewpoints. This flexibility leads to a more profound compassion for others and for myself as I navigate life's complexities. By cultivating an acceptance (or an exploration) of contradictions, I can examine most any topic from various perspectives. Acknowledging these contradictions within myself, rather than being consumed by them, signifies a developmental move. This move allows me to hold these contradictions without being limited by them, without them having a hold on me.

This stance demonstrates my desire (it is a far reach) to simultaneously hold two opposing thoughts or realities without shying away from either. My modest ability to integrate seemingly conflicting ideas is a hallmark of personal development (the trail marker of integration described in chapter 4). For me, this integration is a lifelong negotiation. Not too long ago, my sister died in a car accident. She stopped her car on the interstate behind a line of cars also stopped. However, a driver, not paying attention, slammed into the back of the car she was driving, killing her and critically injuring her daughter. Through many years of many sermons, I know I am to radically forgive the inattentive person who, bluntly, killed my sister. I'm supposed to forgive. However, I am not able to. At least not yet. The gap between what I understand the Gospel teaches and how I feel is a contradiction. The gap represents my tenuous relationship with an essential Christian tenet and the feeling of anger I have. Will I resolve this contradiction? I don't know. I know the contradiction heightens my sense of faith's inherent dissonance. I'd rather live honestly in the dissonance than deny either truth. I believe this is how Bonhoeffer lived, and I have learned from him that such contradiction is consistent with human development, however difficult.

BONHOEFFER AND CONGREGATIONAL PRACTICES

Let's return to Bonhoeffer's experience. He spent a year of study at Union Theological Seminary in New York City (1930–1931). During Bonhoeffer's year at Union, sinful (and evil) anti-Semitism was on the rise, with a steep trajectory in Germany. Though Bonhoeffer wasn't fully articulate concerning his opposition, that would change in the United States.

During his year in New York, Bonhoeffer worshipped at Abyssinian Baptist Church in Harlem with his fellow seminarian, Albert Fisher, an African American. Listening to Rev. Adam Clayton Powell Sr.'s sermons and joining Bible study and other church activities had a big impact on Bonhoeffer's thoughts about the growing, malevolent anti-Semitism in Germany.[9]

In the book *Bonhoeffer's Black Jesus*,[10] author Reggie L. Williams describes how Bonhoeffer's human development led him to defiantly stand against Germany via the influence of Harlem's Black Jesus as represented by the theology of Rev. Powell Sr. and the Abyssinian Baptist Church. Bonhoeffer met a Black Christ, a Black Christ who suffered with African Americans in their struggle against systemic injustice and racial violence—and then resisted.

This interpretation of Christianity centers on a Jesus who identifies with the oppressed. Black Jesus exemplifies resistance against domination, challenging the church's tendency to turn faith into a comfortable practice aligned with worldly power.

Harlem's Black Church, with its vibrant faith and resistance, reshaped Bonhoeffer. Leaving Union Seminary despite faculty pleas, he returned to Germany, determined to build a Christ-centered theology that defied the Nazis' misuse of religion.

However, it is important to acknowledge that Bonhoeffer's experience in Harlem was more nuanced than a simple transformation into a hero. He was shaped by the faith and resistance of the Black Church, but he also offered critiques that may have been influenced by unconscious observations stemming from racism. For instance, during an Easter service at Abyssinian Church in 1931, Bonhoeffer was dismayed to discover that the Church charged an entrance fee. What he didn't realize was that the tickets were free passes for the purpose of reserving a pew.[11] His critique was ill informed.

Furthermore, some may view Bonhoeffer unsympathetically due to his decision to align himself with a murder plot against Hitler instead of pursuing nonviolent forms of resistance.

Nevertheless, Bonhoeffer's encounter with the Abyssinian Baptist Church exposed him to a Christian way of life characterized by courageous resistance against a society that accepted sacrifices to false gods. This experience pulled Bonhoeffer into a life shaped by the liberating power of congregational practices and propelled him into the public arena as a voice against the prevailing evil in Germany.

THE SHADOW SIDE OF CONGREGATIONAL FORMATION

Of course, congregational life does not always function consistently with God's desires for the world. Unfortunately, congregations are sometimes known for, well, being mean. The formative dynamics in a congregation may stray from the possibility of human growth development. Think of Carl Jung's description of the "shadow." Individuals have parts of themselves that contain our hidden desires, instincts, and weaknesses. The shadow can be for the good but more typically is expressed in negative ways. When this occurs, the shadow is composed of what we don't want to admit about ourselves—the traits that we view as shameful or dim. This could include anything from negative personality traits to hidden desires or fears.[12]

Churches and other groups also have shadow aspects. Just like people, churches can have hidden harmful streaks. Sometimes good deeds can be a cover-up for fear or a way to push ideas that actually hurt people.

In the corners of congregational life, there are times when actions, behaviors, or words are used to tamp down underlying fears or to express theology shaped to perpetuate destructive desires. These hidden aspects can hinder the personal growth of members within a congregation. They can diminish certain experiences while imposing harmful norms on others in the faith community.

Consider an eighty-year-old church member. She says, "About a year ago, I had a near-death experience. I died after surgery. The hospital staff brought me back to life. While I was dead, I saw a light. I heard angels. I felt warm. I heard the message, 'Don't let those that harm you vex you. Forgive them.' Last week, I told this story at my church Bible study, and a friend came up to me afterward and told me that I shouldn't tell that story ever again at church."

The eighty-year-old was devastated that this member did not accept her testimony. This inappropriate reprimand led her to a nonprofit support group that honors what the church does not. Our eighty-year-old friend stepped out from the shadow of the church.

More than a generation ago, Philip Rieff wrote the book *The Triumph of the Therapeutic*.[13] He did not mean this to be a good thing. However, consider this. Many of us are more likely to share the deepest aspects of our life with a therapist than we would in a Bible study.

Read the following from a sermon preached by the Presbyterian preacher Rev. William Steele:

> The modern-day church spends all its energy trying to be a successful church. Ask anybody: most church people (including pastors) are continually striving for success. What makes for a successful church? The tacit assumption seems to be that being such a church has to do with good worship and music, with a church-school program likely to attract families, with youth groups, and just at the right moment pastoral care. That is the formula that workshops teach, ministers learn, and congregations live by; a little fellowship, a little caring, a little preaching, a little music, a little education, and a little organization.
>
> And what do you end up with? Churchianity! You end up with an organization called the church. But that's all. Think about it.
>
> Jesus never once said anything about the ingredients of what we call a successful church: nothing about church schools, nothing about choirs, nothing about finance committees, custodians, or buildings.
>
> Jesus never once said anything about the ingredients of what we call a successful church. Instead, he asked us to walk in his footsteps.[14]

Craig Dykstra highlights the stark likeness between the detrimental experiences within congregations and the often-toxic nature of various life arenas. In his analysis, he introduces the concept of "patterns of mutual self-destruction,"[15] asserting that the prevailing success narrative of the United States, coupled with congregations' inability to witness Christ's unconditional, redemptive love, leads both culture and the church to a shared outcome: individuals pushed to their limits and facing emotional, relational, and physical challenges, all the while lacking the spiritual support necessary to navigate an increasingly complex, even dangerous world. We can do better than this. Indeed, the potential for a reversal of this mutual self-destruction exists within the church.

The reversal is not achieved through programs, buildings, or critiquing others' understanding of God. Instead, it is through the proclamation of Christ's life, death, and resurrection by the congregation. This proclamation is carried out through core practices within the congregation, including preaching, teaching, and the care of souls.

Sometimes the most important moments of human development in a congregation happen at the edges of its life. As Hebrews 13:13 says, the resurrected Christ is found "outside the camp." This can happen through preaching, teaching, and care of souls, but often in a covert way that is not widely known by the majority of the congregation.

One woman described her experience of this:

> As a woman, I found there was no place in the church to have honest and safe conversations about womanhood in the church. Realities of being a woman—decisions related to reproduction, lower pay than men, emotional and physical abuse, expectations of being nice and not making trouble—don't come up in most Sunday school curriculums. Where is my growth prioritized?

With her pastor's support, she developed an idea: to create a "church within the church" that would provide a space for these conversations.

If you walk by the coffee shop where ten women are meeting, you might not recognize the conversation as "church talk." But you would be witnessing the formation of a community that is providing space for growth that was not available in the designated church building.

The result: mutual self-development.

A FORMATIVE THEORY OF GOD

Some risk reimagining congregations. Such an adventure prompts reimagining God. Or perhaps it is the other way around. Reimagining

God leads to adventurous congregations. Either way, the results are new ways of thinking and acting about Christian life.

A young adult, let's call him Adam, is a brilliant mathematician. He studies partial differential equations, microlocal analysis, and scattering theory. Adam does not believe Jesus turned water into wine at Cana. But he does believe, "Blessed are those who hunger and thirst for righteousness, for they will be filled" (Matthew 5:6). The Sermon on the Mount is read to him, and he says, "I'm all in."

When Adam attends worship for the first time since high school, an usher greets him ("Are you new?") and hands him a card and a pen. The card lists church activities and a place for him to mark activities for which he would volunteer. The list includes nursery helper, ushering, lawn care, joining the finance committee, and more.

Adam looks at the card and feels (yes, feels) empty. The problem isn't that he has lost his religion. The challenge is that he has not found a congregation vigorous enough to match his scientific curiosity. To turn upside down Robert Kegan's phrase "in over our heads,"[16] Adam finds the church *under* his head.

It would take a reimagined congregation to acknowledge varieties of faith emerging in concert with modern physics, new knowledge about the human brain, equitable social constructs, divergent understandings of human nature, and more.

Picture a reconstructed congregation that offers Adam more than a volunteer card. Instead, dream of a congregation that is a resource for that which matters most in Adam's life.

Adventurous congregations direct attention to the brilliant multiplicity of life. We are not one self. We are many selves in many different life arenas. Best practices don't exist. Life is too complex and contextual. You might find yourself praying in idiosyncratic ways. You are free to ask essential questions (why, still, always, systemic racism?).

Your reimagined congregation serves as a resource about any number of crucial matters: antiracism, parenting, finances, gender justice, vocation, virtue, living with ambiguity, and, for sure, how these matters shape your connection not only to the church but to Christ. This is faith beyond social constructs, even the centered constructs of spirituality and religion; as the author John Green says, "When people ask me if I believe in God, I say I believe around God."[17]

I (Tim) know that this is not an all-or-nothing proposal. Yet, helping the church run isn't the only way to show your faith.

A formative congregation would steadfastly and with no apology support your development as a human being. A reimagined congregation is a resource, a bridge between your faith and your life.

Congregations formed in, say, 1840 can be and are essential to human development. There is not a best model of a congregation whose formative power leads to the redemption of what matters most in life. Thank goodness, thank God, that formative congregations are not franchises. Formative congregations represent many traditions and many different ways of being a church.

Additionally, an increasing number of congregations find that they don't need a building. They don't need volunteers. They go without a strategic plan. They meet at dinner tables, or near a garden, or in a neighbor's basement. In these places, God's dream is not faith in congregational growth. God's dream is how you imagine a life that yet could be.[18]

It's Sunday morning (or Tuesday evening). You are standing in your church. You turn to your left and see a young man. You can't read his mind, so you don't know this. You don't see that he wonders how he will have faith around God. How could you know that he is with you now because he seeks a setting where pondering the mysteries, complexities, and enigma of scattering theory (or is it God?) will no longer vex him? You don't know this about him now. But imagine, here in this place, you soon will.

QUESTIONS FOR REFLECTION

1. Why do congregations spend so much time on operations rather than human development?
2. Have you had life-changing experiences like Dietrich Bonhoeffer? If so, unpack them with yourself or with a trusted person.
3. Thinking of Adam; has science outpaced faith?

NOTES

1. Craig Dykstra, *Growing in the Life of Faith: Education and Christian Practices*, 2nd ed. (Louisville: Geneva Press, 2005), 80–100.
2. Dykstra, *Growing in the Life of Faith*, 2nd ed., 20.
3. Mark Chaves, *Congregations in America* (Cambridge, MA: Harvard University Press, 2004).
4. Sam Liddicott, "Natural Selection: Why Music from Our Childhood Stays with Us," Music Musings and Such, https://www.musicmusingsandsuch.com/musicmusingsandsuch/2017/10/15/feature-natural-selection-why-music-from-our-childhoodstay-with-us# (accessed September 2, 2023).
5. Nayantara Dutta, "Why We Remember Music and Forget Everything Else," *Time*, April 14, 2022, https://time.com/6167197/psychology-behind-remembering-music (accessed September 2, 2023).
6. Wendell Berry, *The Wild Birds* (San Francisco: North Point Press, 1986), 126.
7. *Internet Encyclopedia of Philosophy*, s.v. "Dietrich Bonhoeffer (1906–1945)," https://iep.utm.edu/dietrich-bonhoeffer (accessed October 24, 2023).
8. *Internet Encyclopedia of Philosophy*, "Dietrich Bonhoeffer."
9. William Nunnelley, "Bonhoeffer Saw American Racism during Year of Study at Union Seminary," Samford University, January 9, 2017, https://www.samford.edu/news/2017/01/Bonhoeffer-Saw-American-Racism-During-Year-of-Study-at-Union-Seminary (accessed September 3, 2023).
10. Reggie L. Williams, *Bonhoeffer's Black Jesus: Harlem Renaissance Theology and an Ethic of Resistance* (Waco, TX: Baylor University Press, 2014).
11. Charles Marsh, *Strange Glory: A Life of Dietrich Bonhoeffer* (New York: Vintage, 2014), 127–28.
12. C. G. Jung, *Psychology of the Unconscious* (Mineola, NY: Dover, 1912).
13. Philip Rieff, *The Triumph of the Therapeutic: Uses of Faith after Freud* (Chicago: University of Chicago Press, 1966).
14. Quote from a sermon by Rev. William Steele at First Presbyterian Church in Dearborn, Michigan, September 23, 1990.
15. Dykstra, *Growing in the Life of Faith*, 2nd ed., 86.
16. Robert Kegan, *In Over Our Heads: The Mental Demands of Modern Life* (Cambridge, MA: Harvard University Press, 1994).
17. John Green, *The Anthropocene Reviewed: Essays on a Human-Centered Planet* (New York: Dutton, 2021), 97.
18. Tim Shapiro and Kara Faris, *Divergent Church: The Bright Promise of Alternative Faith Communities* (Nashville: Abingdon Press, 2017).

Chapter 4

Trail Markers
How We Know When We Grow

We are all growing, all the time. While indiscernible, billions of cells are replaced daily, and in eighty to one hundred days, thirty trillion will have replaced—the equivalent of a new you. I (Christina) am stunned when my children press the backs of their heels against the wall in the corner of my closet each year with eager smiles and bated breath as I pencil a mark at the top of their head, full inches higher than just the year before. Physical growth can be quantified and measured in these ways, but what about other forms of growth?

In many Christian communities of faith, we are to grow up in every way into him who is the head, into Christ as described in Ephesians 4:15–16: "Speaking the truth in love, we are to grow up in every way into him who is the head, into Christ, from whom the whole body, joined and knit together by every joint with which it is supplied, when each part is working properly, makes bodily growth and upbuilds itself in love." In doing so, congregations are often well versed in matters of Christian formation and spiritual maturation.

Matters of development are often coupled with developing gifts of the Spirit. The apostle Paul's writing about the fruit of the Spirit found in Galatians 5:22–23 lists the fruit of the Spirit as love, joy, peace, forbearance, kindness, goodness, faithfulness, gentleness, and self-control. While developing these characteristics is certainly related to human development, when setting out to develop this project, two considerations took us in a different direction. First, the Galatians passage outlines outcomes but does not quite get at processes. Our hope with our project is to home in on a process that supports development of these and other outcomes. The second consideration was our core value to contextualize what development means to congregations. It was indeed the case that while engaging in the Formative Power project, congregations named for themselves how qualities like peace seeking and faithful living are defined and achieved in their lives and did so in a myriad of ways.

At times, congregations couple matters of Christian growth with understandings of sanctification. In a commonly understood sense, to participate in sanctification is to take part in processes that set one apart for God's purpose. Therefore, God's people are sometimes said to be sanctified because they are set apart for God's special purposes in the world as referenced in Leviticus: "Consecrate yourselves therefore, and be holy; for I am the LORD your God. Keep my statutes and do them; I am the LORD who sanctifies you" (Leviticus 20:7–8). Here again, sanctification is not separate from development. The pitfall lay within the proclivity of persons to associate the "set-apartness" as somehow extricated from the banal chaos of everyday life. Our intention is to inspire the opposite. We wanted to find ways to frame congregational life as permeating the whole of people's lives.

So, then, what about how we develop as whole human beings?

Insights from human development, also known as developmental psychology, provide an additional lens through which we can understand how humans are formed throughout life. Theories of human development seek to describe predictable patterns of psychological and relational changes as one grows and matures from birth to death. This chapter outlines the third part of the Formative Power of Your Congregation curriculum and employs psychological insights that support the ways communities of faith form people. We offer a description of human development that reflects a joining of holiness and wholeness.[1] To chart this kind of formation we identified eight of what we call trail markers of human development. Each trail marker is supported by key theories of human development that help illuminate how each of these trail markers support individuals in their everyday lives. The eight markers are *attachment, emotional regulation, self-differentiation, initiative, competence, authority, integration,* and *transcendence.*

ATTACHMENT

British psychologist John Bowlby was one of the first attachment theorists. He described attachment as a "lasting psychological connectedness between human beings."[2] Bowlby was interested in understanding the distress that children experience when separated from their primary caregivers. The central theme of attachment theory is that primary caregivers who are available and responsive to an infant's needs allow the child to develop a sense of internalized safety and security. The infant learns that the caregiver is dependable, which creates a secure base for the child to then explore the world. Access to that early dependability endures and often translates into an ability to appropriately depend on self and others.

Many theorists and practitioners have expanded Bowlby's work to extend the impact of relationships beyond primary caregivers and across the life cycle in ways that enhance, and even repair, a person's attachment capacity. Congregations are a prime example of this extension. Our project defines attachment as *the ability to have healthy relationships in which you are your best and truest self. Through positive relationships, you are able to get essential needs like safety, truth telling, forgiveness, and trust met.* We believe that our growth is enhanced through life in community.

For example, we worked with a church that sought to develop its members' capacity to engage in conversations at a deeper level such that they could know and be known by one another. They endeavored to create spaces where honest sharing could also support them in forging connections with the community around them. The members of this congregation were learning to become their best and truest selves through life in community and nurturing more secure attachments.

How might your congregation form more secure attachments in people and how might this transform their lives?

EMOTIONAL REGULATION

Consider the experience of being cut off in traffic by a distracted or otherwise hurried driver. In these moments, a flood of frustration—also known as road rage—can ensue when considering the harm that could have been caused if it were not for the defensive driving of others on the road. It is possible to be swept away by frustration and begin to yell, curse, or even speed up to return the favor. Like standing waist deep along a coastline and being greeted by a cresting wave, exercising emotional regulation allows waves of strong feelings like frustration to rise without the need for an immediate reaction or resistance as it trusts that these waters will eventually recede. What's more, emotional regulation allows for discovery and surprise as we attune to self and other as is, rather than as we wish things to be. In response to a flood of intense frustration on the road, emotional regulation is the capacity to not act reactively but to respond helpfully. Emotional regulation may also include the discovery that the car slowed to a safe speed after the initial swerve, or the self-discovery surprise that part of our frustration was less about the other driver and more about our own diminished patience from not having gotten enough sleep the night before.

An approach to emotional regulation that has gained regard in Western cultures in recent years is mindfulness practices and related skills.[3] Mindfulness helps one learn to "be" in the present moment rather than to ruminate on the past or become preoccupied with the future. It also helps one pay attention to what is happening internally in each passing moment (thoughts, feelings, sensations, and impulses) as well as externally (what we see, hear, smell, and touch) in nonjudgmental and curious ways. Mindfulness skills can help one emotionally regulate by slowing us down enough to name, listen to, and be in relationship with our emotions.[4]

Our project defines emotional regulation as *the capacity to experience, name, express, and act in the midst of positive and painful emotions in a way over which you have agency.* You have emotions; the emotions don't have you. Likewise, you can be in tune with the emotions of others and hold those emotions without being swept away.

Instead of reacting when emotionally laden topics are discussed, emotional regulation enables one to slow down enough to listen, share, be curious, and even be influenced. In one congregational setting, this looked like building the capacity of their membership to discuss divisive topics related to race. By growing in this way, this congregation endeavored to better live out their commitment to racial reconciliation in their own lives and their surrounding communities.

How might your congregation form emotional regulation in people and how might this transform their lives?

SELF-DIFFERENTIATION

Family systems theory is the foundation of family therapy and focuses on the family as a whole that is greater than the sum of its parts. A central tenet of family systems theory is that a family is a unit, and individual behavior can best be understood by considering the context of the larger family. Individuals are influenced by their family, but individuals also influence their family in return. This is the case in congregations as well.

Much of family systems theory is based on the work of Murray Bowen, a psychiatrist who developed the theory. According to Bowen, family systems theory relies on individuals developing self-differentiation, the ability to maintain individuality and connectedness simultaneously.

Later, Edwin Howard Friedman, an ordained rabbi and family therapist born in 1932, focused a great deal of his career on self-differentiation in religious contexts. His seminal work *Generation to Generation* was written for leaders of religious congregations and focuses on leaders developing three main areas of themselves—being self-differentiated, nonanxious, and present with those one is leading.[5]

Our project draws on these principles of growth for all within congregations and defines self-differentiation as *the ability to experience oneself as separate from others, or to "differentiate" oneself, with personal values, thoughts, feelings, and choices, while at the same time remaining in relationship with those who are in any number of ways distinct from you.*

One of the congregations we worked with engaged self-differentiation as a trail marker of growth. This community sought to normalize struggles with anxiety and to provide tools and resources to develop self-differentiation. They endeavored to help members cope with their anxiety and not let the anxiety of others unduly affect them. In doing so, this congregation supported the growth and development of individuals through retreats and storytelling and experienced formation of new kinds.

How might your congregation form self-differentiation in people and how might this transform their lives?

INITIATIVE

Erik Erikson entered the field of developmental psychology at a transitional point in its theoretical history—a shift from focusing on interior motivations that dominated explanations of human behavior to including the influence of one's environment on development. His psychosocial development sought to address the demands the relational context places on development. In Erikson's theory of psychosocial development, each stage presented its own developmental opportunity in response to changes in social interactions and new relationships that develop with age.[6]

In one such development opportunity, Erikson described crossroads between initiative and guilt. Here he outlines concerns about the capacity to assert one's power in the world through play and other social interactions with others. Success in this stage instills a sense of being capable of various forms of leadership, whereas failure results in struggles with guilt, self-doubt, and lack of initiative in life.[7]

Our project builds on Erickson's appreciation for growing in this way and defines the trail marker of initiative as *the ability to be resourceful in relationship to the challenges and opportunities faced in life. One is not passive but uses creativity and talents to accomplish goals and help others to be proactive as well.* In other words, we understand initiative as the capacity to develop one's voice as a source of influence in the world.

One congregation engaged this trail marker by increasing their degree of risk taking involved in living out their mission to its fullest. Over the long term, they could see how this area of growth would lend itself to renewed energy and a revised vision for their congregation, as well as enhance the capacity to live out of abundance rather than scarcity in their lives. They also saw how such an area of development was connected to congregants adopting formal leadership positions within their congregation and beyond.

How might your congregation form initiative in people and how might this transform their lives?

COMPETENCE

Jean Piaget's cognitive human development model proposes that each individual psyche contains the seeds of flourishing as a genetic inheritance, but reaching full potential requires stimulation from the environment—that is, cognitive development is experiential.[8] He outlined aspects of cognitive development that span from childhood to adulthood, including gaining the capacity to think in various abstract, hypothetical, and systematic terms.[9] Piaget's work highlights that we never stop learning and that our environment, including the people therein, shapes the nature and degree of cognitive growth.

We also know that cognitive competence is but one of many ways of "knowing." There are a multitude of intelligences that can be shaped and developed by one's environment. Our project defines competence broadly as *identifying and developing one's skills and gifts. Such ability applies to numerous life arenas including school, households, vocation, civic life, and family. Competency involves learning how to do certain activities and how to think strategically about situations and systems.*

One church fostered the formation of competency in their members by shifting the way their congregation understood their sense of calling in the world. To do so, they learned together about biblical references to, and the multiple meanings of, reconciliation. The learning served as a primer for congregants to be able to engage in conversations on race differently, equipped with new concepts and theological language. Additionally, this congregation embraced expert-led cultural competency training with the object of promoting positive engagement with racialized systems. Increasing competency was vital to this faith community's growth and development.

How might your congregation form competence in people and how might this transform their lives?

AUTHORITY

Carol Gilligan was a psychologist best known for her innovative views on the development of women's morality and sense of self. She detailed her views in the 1982 book *In a Different Voice,* in which she argues that the highest level of moral development is postconventional morality. At the postconventional level, the needs of the self are just as important as the needs of others, which causes an individual to arrive at a universal ethic of care and concern.[10] Gilligan believed in adhering to the obligation of care, while avoiding harm to or exploitation of oneself and others, and accepting responsibility for one's own choices.

Building on Gilligan's ethic of care, we define authority as *the experience of seeing others as equal and mutual, especially authority figures. It involves being able to "own" one's power and acknowledge the authority of others in ways that don't diminish oneself.*

A wonderful example of mutual authority grew out of a collaboration between two congregational leaders who participated in the Formative Power curriculum together. These two leaders, one Black and one white, created a podcast through which they could amplify both of their voices and have honest dialogues about social justice in the Bible. This collaboration not only modeled friendship among equals, but it explicitly called forth increased authority and responsibility within those listening. You will meet these leaders in chapter 5.

How might your congregation form authority in people and how might this transform their lives?

INTEGRATION

Object relations theory developed during the late 1920s and the 1930s and became important in shaping psychoanalytic theory during the 1970s. Donald Winnicott, Margaret Mahler, and Melanie Klein are among those credited with its origination and refinement. Within this developmental theory, an external object can be a person, a thing, or an experience. And at times these people, things, or experiences can be tolerated only in part—for example, only seeing the good in a caregiver, or on the other hand only seeing the bad. However, to accept integrated whole objects is to accept a person, thing, or experience more fully and as they actually are, with all their positive and negative traits. According to object relations theory, if we successfully move through these stages of development, we are able to relate to others and the world as more integrated wholes and more as they truly are.

Integration of good and bad, or at least how good or bad things seem, can be particularly challenging for faith communities where questions of theodicy have been debated for years. Namely, how can a good God allow bad things to happen? While we consider there to be a range of faithful responses to this question, for the purposes of our project we define integration less theologically and more experientially as *the experience of reconciling negative aspects of life, such as losses, imperfection, sin, and pain, along with the positive aspects of life, such as love, purpose, and accomplishment.*

An illustrative example of a congregation that formed its people's capacity for integration was a church with a program that centered on the importance of knowing one's family history and the joy of scrapbooking. With the help of the Indiana Public Library and the Indiana Historical Society, participants were able to collect their own researched artifacts and create their own scrapbooks on a selected topic. Through this process, church members would build capacity for integration by holding together the good, the bad, and everything in between that constitutes family histories.

How might your congregation form integration in people and how might this transform their lives?

TRANSCENDENCE

Theologian and human development professor James Fowler was a minister in the United Methodist Church and is best known for his book *Stages of Faith*, published in 1981. He sought to develop the idea of a developmental process in "human faith."[11] Among the later stages of faith development that he described was "conjunctive" faith. This stage acknowledges paradox and transcendence relating to the reality behind the symbols of inherited systems. At this stage, an individual resolves conflicts from previous stages by a complex understanding of a multidimensional, interdependent "truth" that cannot be explained by any statement. In other words, truth is an experience and is bigger, and more transcendent, than our words can contain.

For the purpose of this project, we expand upon Fowler's understanding and appreciation for transcendence and define it as *the realization that life is larger than oneself, that one is part of a reality greater than the self, and the experience of finding and contributing to meaning, purpose, and ultimate concerns beyond oneself.*

One congregation we worked with made it their aim to promote experiences of transcendence by helping people come to know that the life of the church extends far beyond formal worship experiences on Sunday. They did so by engaging their aging membership in arts-related activities throughout the week. This practice simultaneously reflected and reinforced that the congregation and the mission of the church is deeply committed to each individual, regardless of age or stage in life, living life to the utmost fullness with passion, zeal, and the love of others.

How might your congregation form transcendence in people and how might this transform their lives?

CONTEMPORARY AND PASTORAL REFLECTIONS ON HUMAN DEVELOPMENT

While human development models offer a great deal of insight to be applied to the markers of formation that occur in congregations, there are a few important ways they are not always helpful. First, contemporary pastoral theology does not view social environment as an obstacle. On the contrary, this text is a testament to communities being an essential conduit of development. Growth is not understood as occurring despite but rather chiefly *because of* the social environment. Growth is relationally driven. Allan Schore, a leading researcher on the developmental aspects of brain neurobiology, asserts that the child's future social and emotional development, including the actual structure of the brain, is determined by the primary caregiver having significant responsibility as a mediator for that environment.[12] Thus, cognitive and emotional development and neurological maturation are not separate processes but are intertwined. Growth in all areas is intrinsically dependent on relationships. It is not too much to say that the brain itself is shaped by social and emotional relations from birth.[13]

Historically, development was conceived of as occurring in linear stages. At the completion of one stage, the individual moves on to the next stage. Traditional concepts of psychopathology are often related to whether someone has achieved a normative standard for development. However, this kind of stage-oriented view of human development has cultural as well as theological implications. There are many contextual variations to what is considered normative. For example, certain cultures emphasize certain cognitive capacities over others. Additionally, stage-oriented theories do not consider nonlinear concepts of human growth. For pastoral theology, this means considering human development according to kairos (God's Divine timing not marked by past, present, or future) rather than *chronos* (ordinary, chronological, and sequential time). Kairos time makes room for God's role in when and how development happens.

Pamela Cooper-White engages these three areas of human development critique in her article "Human Development in Relational and Cultural Perspective."[14] She argues that human development occurs as a "complex, organic and intrinsically relational human phenomenon." Drawing on insights from object relations theory, family systems thinking, neurology, biology, sociocultural criticism, and theology, she concludes that growth occurs through simultaneous cycles of development, including the overarching dimension of time—both linear and eternal.[15] These multiple exchanges across linear (*chronos*) and eternal (*kairos*) time consequently impact individuals' developing sense of themselves as created in the image of God and able to effect change in the world as well as their sense of interconnectedness with creation.

Identifying trail markers of human development helps answer the question of the relationship between spiritual maturity and relational maturity by conveying that perhaps they are one thing, not two different issues after all. The relationships fostered in congregations help form our character so profoundly because of how profoundly we are all shaped by who we love. Development happens best for us when we are helpfully connected to others who demonstrate new possibilities for our lives and for what we offer to others. Such is the formative power of congregations.

NOTES

1. Les L. Steele, *On the Way: A Practical Theology of Christian Formation* (Eugene: Wipf and Stock, 1998).
2. John Bowlby, *Attachment and Loss* (New York: Basic Books, 1969).
3. Albert Feliu-Soler, Juan C. Pascual, Xavier Borràs, Maria J. Portella, Ana Martín-Blanco, Antonio Armario, Enric Alvarez, Victor Pérez, and Joaquim Soler, "Effects of Dialectical Behaviour Therapy–Mindfulness Training on

Emotional Reactivity in Borderline Personality Disorder: Preliminary Results," *Clinical Psychology & Psychotherapy* 21, no. 4 (March 2013): 363–70, https://doi.org/10.1002/cpp.1837.

4. Marianne Goodman, David Carpenter, Cheuk Y. Tang, Kim E. Goldstein, Jennifer Avedon, Nicolas Fernandez, Kathryn A. Mascitelli, et al., "Dialectical Behavior Therapy Alters Emotion Regulation and Amygdala Activity in Patients with Borderline Personality Disorder," *Journal of Psychiatric Research* 57 (October 2014): 108–16, https://doi.org/10.1016/j.jpsychires.2014.06.020.

5. Edwin H. Friedman, *Generation to Generation: Family Process in Church and Synagogue* (New York: Guilford, 1985).

6. Lee H. Butler Jr., *Liberating Our Dignity, Saving Our Souls: A New Theory of African American Identity Formation* (St. Louis: Chalice Press, 2006), 89.

7. Felicity Kelcourse, *Human Development and Faith: Life-Cycle Stages of Body, Mind, and Soul*, 2nd ed. (St. Louis: Chalice Press, 2015), 35.

8. Kelcourse, *Human Development*, 38.

9. Kelcourse, *Human Development*, 39.

10. Carol Gilligan, "In a Different Voice: Women's Conceptions of Self and of Morality," *Harvard Educational Review* 47, no. 4 (1977): 481–517, https://doi.org/10.17763/haer.47.4.g6167429416hg5l0.

11. Nancy J. Evans, Deanna S. Forney, Florence M. Guido, Lori D. Patton, and Kristen A. Renn, *Student Development in College: Theory, Research, and Practice*, 2nd ed. (San Francisco: Jossey-Bass, 2010).

12. Allan N. Schore, "Effects of a Secure Attachment Relationship on Right Brain Development, Affect Regulation, and Infant Mental Health," *Infant Mental Health Journal* 22 (January 2003): 7–66, https://doi.org/10.1002/1097-0355(200101/04)22:1%3C7::AID-IMHJ2%3E3.0.CO;2-N.

13. Evans et al., 97.

14. Pamela Cooper-White, "Human Development in Relational and Cultural Perspective," in *Human Development and Faith: Life-Cycle Stages of Body, Mind and Soul* (St. Louis: Chalice Press, 2004), 80–102.

15. Cooper-White, 94.

PART II
Stories of Formation

Chapter 5

Forming People of Racial Reconciliation

Let's begin this chapter with an introduction to Essie Payne.

Essie Payne was a member of Westminster Presbyterian Church, a congregation I (Tim) served for fourteen years. An African American woman, Essie was raised by her mother in the hills of Ohio. As an adult, she moved from the hills to Wilberforce, Ohio. She attended worship every Sunday. Essie served as an elder and a chair of several committees and led a parenting group that involved almost ninety people: church members who were parents, foster parents, family court judges, social workers, high school counselors, recently incarcerated women seeking to reunite with their sons or daughters, fathers in twelve-step groups, and even the mayor of Xenia, Ohio. After many years of writing and teaching at Central State University, she published her memoir, *Mama and the Hills of Home*.[1]

In her memoir, Essie describes that the leaders of the high school she attended awarded a full scholarship to the valedictorian each year, typically to attend Wilmington College, a Quaker school. The year of her graduation, Essie earned the highest grades in her class, which meant she earned the position of valedictorian and the scholarship.

However, the principal made clear to Essie that she would not be valedictorian and would not receive the scholarship. Essie repeatedly reached out to the principal, but to no avail. She contacted Wilmington College and received a vague but telling response: no.

Essie knew that she was not awarded the scholarship because she was a Black woman.

When Essie told me this story and I read about it in more detail in her book, I thought to myself, "My goodness, the church must be one of the few places she could feel safe." Essie, a strong and resilient woman, would likely not say the words I thought. Her mother had taught her self-respect and tenacity. Yet, still, I feel my impression to be true.

For many Black people, the church has historically been one of the few public places where they could feel at home, where they could feel that there was no clear and present danger.[2]

Therefore, it was gratifying that many congregations in the Formative Program acknowledged the Black Church's reassuring presence for Black people, even though this need is a result of racism. It was inspiring when several congregations went further than being satisfied with the church being a safe place for people of color. They explored ways that churches can be agents for social justice. In recent years, there has been a growing movement to address racial injustice, perhaps a long-awaited rediscovery within churches.[3]

Congregations of color, who for too long have experienced the tragic effects of racism, have led the movement. Black Churches, Spanish-speaking, immigrant, and multicultural congregations, and more are all too familiar with the life arena of racism perpetuated by white churches and other power structures. Nonwhite congregations have lived with racism's effects for generations. They have a hard-earned authority to speak about such.

Leaders of the Black Church are called upon time and time again to explain individual and systemic racism to white people. The task is tiring, not because the job isn't essential but because the effort is endless.

Many members of white churches have been slow to embrace this movement, often due to participants' fear of experiencing the discomfort that prods repentance. For many churches with primarily white congregants, the need for racial justice and the need to acknowledge complicity in racism is a difficult, unwanted way of thinking. Some congregants initially react defensively. Yet the same congregants, as they experienced uncomfortable situations or revelatory teachings, grow and see that racism is a tragic reality that must be addressed.

TWO CONGREGATIONS

This chapter tells the story of two congregations, New Era Church and Common Ground Church. The former congregation is predominantly Black, and the latter is primarily white.

The two churches, led by their pastors, began a journey of truth telling and repentance, guided by hope. The two pastors, Dr. Clarence Moore and Pastor Jeff Krajewski, explored the reality of racial injustice together, culminating in worshipping as one on at least three occasions. As a result, they grew in several areas, including emotional self-regulation and integrating the truth of finding one's voice regarding racism.

Common Ground Church is twenty years old. The work of racial justice is new to this congregation. However, Pastor Jeff and many members are committed to learning and growing as Christians. The desire for lifelong learning, particularly about essential matters of life, has led members of Common Ground to conversations about race and privilege, discussions leading to new thought patterns and new, kindred relationships.

When Pastor Jeff was talking with Common Ground lay leaders about his call to the church, he made it clear that if he was called as pastor, he would proclaim the gospel of justice. He wanted to be clear with the laity and perhaps by doing so seal the covenant within himself.

New Era Church is seventy-seven years old. The church is the result of a merger between Northside and New Era, hence its name until about ten years ago: Northside New Era Church (now New Era). Dr. Moore is the long-tenured pastor.

At the time of the merger, the Northside congregation had a building but no pastor. The Northside congregation had purchased a building from a Methodist Church in 1939, a congregation in which members were participating in white flight from the neighborhood to one of the early suburbs of Indianapolis.

Once on the property, members of what used to be the Northside Church discovered various items associated with the Ku Klux Klan, the hate group with strong historical ties to Indiana, on the church's premises.

Indiana was once congested with the Ku Klux Klan, particularly during the early 1900s, hosting one of the nation's largest Klan memberships. The Klan's oath openly endorsed racist and white supremacist beliefs, asserting the diabolic superiority of white Protestants' race and religion.[4]

The Klan's presence in Indiana brought disgrace to the state, as its members terrorized African Americans and other marginalized groups without consequence. However, in recent decades, the Klan's influence in Indiana has significantly diminished.

Nevertheless, white congregations need to know this depraved history. You cannot participate in redemption without knowing and holding the truth.

Now, did the Methodists, the previous occupants of the building, know about this? Were they complicit? Or were they dangerously naive? I don't know.

Regardless, New Era does not keep these discoveries from decades past a secret. The congregation's presence on this land is a holy reclamation. The fact that the congregation exists on property once occupied by the Ku Klux Klan is testimony to Christ's victory over systemic evil. The property represents a promised land ethic for the congregation. No wonder the congregation claims the name New Era.

Dr. Moore muses, "Perhaps this site could be a designated landmark someday."

THE LIFE ARENA OF SOCIAL JUSTICE

A highlight of the experience between the two congregations is the relationship between the two pastors. New Era Church's Dr. Moore mentors Pastor Jeff Krajewski, offering guidance on combating racism. Their now well-established friendship, secured through faith, is a testament to their commitment to solidarity.

In some Formative Power efforts, the church's energy toward formation sometimes comes from adherents. Sometimes, as in this case, the power for growth begins with the clergypersons. The maturity of the minister becomes the opening for the growth of participants.

Many pastors are wary of serving as exemplars, and for good reason. Clergy frequently deal with projections of parishioners' fears upon them.

- Aren't we about spiritual matters?

- I don't even know what you mean by social justice.
- Can't we just stick to strengthening the congregation?

A crucial meeting between Dr. Moore and Pastor Jeff occurred at a Formative Power meeting. The subject of the class was life arenas. Participants discussed a long list including parenting, vocation, art, and more.

Note that the class was not about church property, ushers, or the proper shade of orange for the nursery carpet. No, the class was about faith and life.

Halfway through the class, the group's attention turned to social justice, particularly the reality of racism. And participants described racism differently.

A Lutheran pastor framed racism in terms of systemic racism. He said, "Racism ruins communities and institutions. My parents grew up in a town where the Black school did not have a gymnasium. The white school had a gymnasium and a swimming pool."

A Presbyterian pastor said, "Social justice is buried. As a Black minister, I take Paul seriously. The dangerous reality of principalities and powers privilege white people and disadvantage my parents and children."

A Roman Catholic priest said succinctly, "My ethics teacher would say that racism is the incredulous belief that white people are superior to Black people."

You probably hear the sad refrain: "Sunday-morning church is the most segregated time in American life."[5]

Pastor Jeff is in the classroom. He feels his heart, soul, and mind (are they different?) stirred, even agitated, by the conversation.

Here is a crucial moment: Pastor Jeff turns to the person sitting to his right and says, "If I use the phrase 'social justice' in my religious circle, people will have no idea what I'm talking about."

The person next to Pastor Jeff is Dr. Moore. He says to Pastor Jeff, "Let's the two of us get together."

ATTACHMENT AS MUTUAL TRUST

Pastor Jeff and Dr. Moore began a series of conversations about racism in the United States and the North American church. Dr. Moore is direct about racism: "It's everywhere, and the white church must receive the truth."

Dr. Moore is committed to his relationship with Pastor Jeff, and Pastor Jeff wants to learn more. So the two continue discussions, however challenging they may be for Pastor Jeff, over several months.

Dr. Moore and Pastor Jeff share a deep connection rooted in mutual respect as a result of their commitment to their relationship which they have nurtured through ongoing discussions over several months. This deep bond represents the trail marker of secure attachment. Their collaboration has evolved into a genuine friendship, founded on a shared sense of fondness and appreciation for each other.

It is unfortunate that the phrase "mutual affection" is used mostly in the context of romantic or family relationships. When two people are dedicated to an endeavor that is essential to them and entire social systems, there develops a bond complementing and even transcending cognition and intellectual understanding. Between the two an emotional connection develops that is beyond respect. Their relationship represents mutual affection.

And there are other signs of their secure attachment with one another:

- the ability to regulate their emotions in the relationship
- feeling like they have an impact on the world around them
- the capacity to reflect on how they are being in the relationship
- willingness to bond with and trust each other

THE TRAIL MARKER OF INTEGRATION

You may recall that the trail marker of integration refers to the process of unifying the positive and negative aspects of life, such as love and loss, success and failure, joy and sorrow. It is about accepting and embracing all of our experiences, both good and bad, as part of our journey.

Pastor Jeff proclaims the grace of Christ. He knows the good the church can do. He has witnessed the Good News of the Gospel individually and vibrantly at Common Ground Church and in his own life. Yet Pastor Jeff knew he needed to live as a person of faith holding both the church's contribution to the positive formation of people and the church's complicity in racism both long ago and in the current moment.

Pastor Jeff read *The Color of Compromise* by Jemar Tisby. The book's central message is that the white church in America has historically played a role in perpetuating racism and has also provided theological support for discrimination.

In the book's foreword, Lecrae Moore argues that American Christianity has been more than just complicit in racism but has actively promoted it. The word "complicity" suggests that white congregation members have stood by and done nothing. The author states that Christianity has been the driving force behind racism.[6]

Let's return to the resilient Essie Payne introduced above. When I (Tim) was pastor at Westminster Presbyterian Church in Xenia, Ohio, I led a children's sermon one Sunday. I was not prepared (no excuse). Without anything better to do, I asked the children if they had a favorite animal. The answers came easily: a dog named Oscar, two goldfish without names, a rabbit named Bunny.

Our household had a cat, a rescue cat (before the language was used). The cat's name was Integration. When I told the children (and the rest of the congregation) that we had a cat named Integration, the laughter came from the pews. I thought nothing of it. Actually, I oddly liked the cat's name, perhaps as a personal affirmation of school integration.

On Monday, I was reading in my office when Essie Payne came into the study. Essie said to me, "You did something yesterday that was without a doubt wrong, and what is worse is I don't think you think you did anything wrong."

I didn't know what possible wrong Essie could be referring to.

Essie said, "When you said your cat was named Integration, the congregation *laughed*. My brother and sisters, literally, my brothers and sisters still are blocked from living in neighborhoods with whites. And Black people who find a way to live where they choose, just like you, have paid a price higher than you will ever know."

She continued: "If you remember, I was denied a scholarship because a high school and a college were categorically against anything close to integration."

My apology that followed was shallow compared to Essie's truth. The apology wasn't nearly enough. I'm still unsure what unadorned repentance is.

It turns out that the church wasn't a safe place for Essie after all.

Tisby writes, "History and Scripture teach us that there can be no reconciliation without repentance. There can be no repentance without confession. And there can be no confession without truth."[7]

Applying the truth from Dr. Moore's theological convictions and his quickly growing imperative to tell the truth, Pastor Jeff preaches on social justice. At Common Ground, one of his sermons is based on Matthew 20. The text proclaims that Jesus emptied himself. In white power structures, Pastor Jeff notes, "we should not grasp for power. We can empty ourselves."

Remember that in this text, Jesus calls disciples to him and says, "You know that the rulers of the Gentiles lord it over them, and their great ones are tyrants over them. It will not be so among you; but whoever wishes to be great among you must be your servant, and whoever wishes to be first among you must be your slave; just as the Son of Man came not to be served but to serve, and to give his life as a ransom for many" (Matthew 20:25–28).

One difficulty with the passage is the use of the word "slave" (*doulos*) by the Matthew community. *Doulos* literally translates to "slave," which evokes images of the oppressive institution of slavery. However, there are other interpretations of the word, and it is possible that the Matthew community was using it in a more figurative sense.[8]

The use of the word is problematic for the very reason that we do not know the exact intention of the original use, and we do know the transgression of enslavement. Writing "transgression" instead of "sin" is intentional because "transgression" is a stronger word (at least for me) because it denotes a sense of knowingly and deliberately crossing moral or ethical boundaries, implying a more deliberate or willful act than the word "sin."

You may be bought and sold and bought, but that makes you first among us.

Yet this is not what Pastor Jeff teaches. Pastor Jeff refers to an emptying that results in devotion to another so as to disregard one's own interests. From a white privilege perspective, the passage becomes a directive for white people to diligently and willingly renew their minds regarding race, both in terms of complicity and intentionality.

How? By giving up pretentions of power. Congregations that address racism do so because they are mentored by people or have experienced congregational activities that are intentionally designed to challenge prejudice and the power dynamics that sustain it.

Now, much of the mutual affection between Dr. Moore and Pastor Jeff developed via conversation. They shared their thoughts, beliefs, and personal experiences openly and honestly. These discussions were not merely exchanges of words; they were opportunities for them to connect more deeply than the typical mundane talk of everyday life.

In the following section, we will listen in on what Dr. Moore and Pastor Jeff shared with one another. Their comments represent how meaningful dialogue can transcend differences and illuminate the transformative potential of conversations centered on crucial matters of faith.

THE POWER OF RELIGIOUS CONVERSATION

So, meeting time and time again, Dr. Moore speaks Gospel truths. Let us hear a compilation of their conversations. First, Dr. Moore speaks:

> Jesus and justice are synonymous. Justice is sought in the political arena. Yet justice is also a spiritual issue. People tag justice as a purely political issue. That's a copout. It is too easy to say that justice is a political issue and not a matter for the church. Racial justice is a spiritual, moral value. It transcends politics. Did you hear the announcement at the Wilberforce University graduation? Financial debts to the university would be forgiven! One of the significant "donors" was the United Negro College Fund. Funds also came from emergency relief funds [the CARES Act].

It is worth noting that Wilberforce is a historically Black college representing the African Methodist Episcopal tradition (five miles from Xenia, Ohio).

Now, Dr. Moore observes that racial injustice is also revealed in micro, everyday interactions. A white coworker talks about a colleague: "He has a dark heart." Think about it: why is the word "dark" used? Pastor Jeff knows that Dr. Moore speaks Gospel truth. How? Pastor Jeff works and prays to live the way of life created by Jesus Christ. His mind is open to Dr. Moore's hard-earned wisdom because Dr. Moore is providing a front door by which Pastor Jeff can lead his congregation to the life arena of social justice.

So, let's listen to Pastor Jeff:

> I'm hearing an ongoing theme that race is a made-up social construct that is used to continually create a power dynamic based on skin color, and that it is a social construct perpetuated, in many ways, by the church. That is why we read *The Color of Compromise*; the church has been complicit in both constructing that system in America but also theologically supporting it, and we as Christians have a responsibility to learn, repent, turn around, do something different in regard to our complicity and racism. Now we have a theological responsibility, not just a social responsibility.

Remember our earlier exploration of Jürgen Habermas's view of unlimited conversation? The conversations between Dr. Moore and Pastor Jeff do have a never-ending quality. There is always more to say. There is always more to be learned. In fact, the two clergymen have created a podcast called *Shades of Hope*, thirty-five episodes and counting described as a frank conversation between two friends who make the case for racial justice within the Gospel.[9]

THE TRAIL MARKER OF SELF-REGULATION

Some conversations are difficult. The change of heart and soul and the renewal of minds are always challenging, particularly in churches, which often domesticate the Gospel into trite wisdom sayings. Once, I was in a conversation with an officeholder about the churches in town hoping for a town meeting about addiction. He said, "I don't think we need a town meeting; people just need to do the work of Jesus Christ. Jesus told us all we need to know: Early to bed, early to rise makes a man healthy, wealthy, and wise."

We know that conversations of candor require more than wrongly attributed and time-worn wisdom sayings.[10]

A gentleman is talking to Pastor Jeff. The gentleman says, cynically, that he grew up in hard times, and he made it through without special help. Pastor Jeff listens quietly and patiently. He does not interrupt or try to correct the gentleman. He holds the space for the gentleman to talk.

After a while, the gentleman says, "To be honest, to be fair, I don't have any relationships with people of color I can have this conversation with."

The conversation could have gone differently. Jeff might have sternly corrected the person. The parishioner might have chosen to walk out. Neither happened. The discussion reflected the theme in 1 John 4 of love over fear.

Staying engaged in complex conversations requires emotional monitoring. In family systems theory, self-regulation (also a trail marker) is the capacity to experience, name, express, and act amid positive and painful emotions over which you have agency.[11]

You have feelings. The emotions don't have you. Likewise, you can be in tune with the feelings of others and hold those emotions without being swept away.[12]

On another occasion, Jeff sits with a woman, a former military member. She participates in small-group conversation about racism and justice. Pastor Jeff asks, "What is it like?"

"An awakening," she says.

She calls her experience an awakening because she, being sympathetic, learned how all-encompassing racial disparity is.

"How was I unaware that we swim in such racialized waters?"

LIMINAL EXPERIENCES

Common Ground congregants discuss possible trips to Selma, Birmingham, and Montgomery, Alabama. They are particularly interested in the Equal Justice Initiative (EJI) led by Bryan Stevenson, which operates the Legacy Museum and the National Memorial for Peace and Justice.[13]

Congregational pilgrimages to previously unknown places provide experiences that disorient inaccurate notions while opening one to revelation, even transcendence, a force, a divinity, an unveiled hope beyond oneself. So often, human development flourishes when one relinquishes control, when someone else is directing the experience and you are not.

The EJI is a nonprofit organization that works to end mass incarceration and excessive punishment in the United States. The Legacy Museum tells the story of slavery, lynching, and segregation in America. The National Memorial for Peace and Justice memorializes the victims of racial terror lynchings in the United States.

The congregants believe that a pilgrimage to these places would be a powerful experience to help them understand the history of racism in America.

The Common Ground congregants are right. Pilgrimages to previously unknown places can be disorienting but can also be revelatory.

When we relinquish control and allow someone else to direct our experience, we allow ourselves to be surprised and transformed. We are opening ourselves up to the possibility of growing and accepting the transformative power of living so that love ultimately overwhelms fear. We called such congregational activities "liminal space" within the Formative Power design.

The word "liminal" has become increasingly popular in the past decade. This surge in usage could reflect a deeper human yearning to transcend the limitations of our social constructs. These constructs, often focused on prescribed life paths like "grow up, get married, get a job," can feel increasingly narrow in a rapidly changing world. This rigidity might serve the needs of the economic machine, but it risks stifling the human desire for experiences that exist beyond the self.

Thankfully, the rise of "liminal" isn't just a trend; it's a reclamation of our yearning for experiences that transcend the confines of our daily lives. Liminal theology reflects this desire, embracing the transformative potential of stepping outside our comfort zones. By venturing into the liminal space, we open ourselves to the mysteries inherent in faith and human development.

For Pastor Jeff, preaching antiracism wasn't easy, but he wasn't afraid to challenge the status quo. He understood that addressing racism required not just outward actions but also a willingness to reexamine long-held beliefs. By incorporating antiracism themes into his sermons and encouraging reflection on faith, he pushed his congregation to confront their biases. This approach, akin to venturing into uncharted territory, demonstrated commitment to creating a more just community. For Common Ground, formation involved growth in self-differentiation, the ability to be in a relationship with another, and honoring the other's self while not giving away oneself.[14]

At the end of the movie *Little Man Tate* (about a boy who doesn't fit in established social structures), the narrator (Tate himself) says, "Only when all who surround you are different will you truly belong."[15]

In a congregation that has yet to succumb to being a membership society, the formation field can grow around the most important and challenging life arenas. Formation involves thinking about how people change and grow. For example, Pastor Jeff's thinking about social justice led to an entire congregation thinking and acting humbly about antiracism. Prior thoughts were juxtaposed with new ways of thinking. Such self-reflection about thinking is essential to faith development and growth as human beings.

Remember that Emmanuel Levinas states that we come to know one another face-to-face. A woman bravely confesses to another that she had no idea racism was steadfastly systemic. A man, defensive at first, notices how closely Pastor Jeff is listening. Dr. Moore and Pastor Jeff break bread face-to-face. For Levinas, the human face is the conduit of God.[16]

PILGRIMAGES AS CONGREGATIONAL ACTIVITIES

Congregations take trips. Some of the travel is focused on fellowship. Some congregational treks are educational. Some are mission trips.

In the Formative Program, we think of all sorts of trips as pilgrimages. We've noticed that when congregation members travel together, it becomes more than a regular outing. It becomes a chance for everyone to connect with their faith and be pushed out of their comfort zones by trying new things. These pilgrimages are all about sharing beliefs and experiences. It's like a spiritual adventure where everyone learns something new about themselves and what they believe.

As a teenager, Pastor Jeff traveled to Chicago with his youth group. These trips made a lasting impression, one that may very well have grounded his interest in social justice as an adult. The trips were initiated by Rev. Wayne Gordon (now Dr. Wayne "Coach" Gordon), Pastor Jeff's youth pastor.[17]

Pastor Jeff recalls that Rev. Gordon worked with Dr. John Perkins to launch the Christian Community Development Association. "Before this, Rev. Gordon led a little church on the South Side of Chicago in the Lawndale community, and so we would get in a very dangerous church van (I would want to make sure the back-escape door worked) and drive up to Lawndale."[18]

The church in Lawndale hosted a housing project where they would acquire abandoned houses, rehabilitate them, and move families into those houses to create stability in the neighborhood.

Lawndale sponsored a medical clinic, and the congregation met there for worship. Jeff and his church friends slept in this worship site on the floor. He remembers walking to and from the worksite every day. Jeff was with his friends from the mostly affluent Zionsville, a suburb of Indianapolis. Here he found himself walking through the inner city of Chicago when that particular neighborhood was in disorder. The community had been devastated by crime and drugs, and for the young Jeff Krajewski, this was a first glimpse into the world being skewed to those with advantages not available to others. Jeff worshipped on Sundays with the people from the neighborhood, thinking about the stark contrast between their experiences and his own. He realized that something was wrong, that this wasn't right.

The pilgrimage into liminal space (Zionsville to Chicago) provided Jeff, before he was a pastor, with a path identified in the letter to the Romans, a renewal of one's mind.

A common theme of human development as it relates to congregational life is that people learn to how to look inward and really think about what their thoughts mean. Robert Kegan, a researcher in human development, calls this thinking about thinking.[19]

Thinking about thinking is "metacognition," which is the ability to reflect on one's thinking process. Kegan believes that metacognition is essential for adult development, as it allows us to become more aware of our assumptions and limitations. Such a dynamic describes what occurred (and is occurring) at Common Ground. Recall the man and woman who talked with Pastor Jeff about society and racism. Yes, their feelings of being overwhelmed by the knowledge of white people's advantages in daily life existed. Yet, more than that, their thinking about their previous thoughts about racism was changing via participation in Common Ground.

Pastor Jeff spent hours thinking about how he had been mulling over theology and social justice. He read books he hadn't read before. When Pastor Jeff talked with the angry member who was resisting the church considering racism, Pastor Jeff noted, "I've thought these thoughts too."

Transcendence is the experience of rising above oneself to a better state. It is part of metacognition, which is thinking about one's thinking. Many congregational activities can lead to transcendence, such as being swept away by the music on Easter morning, the imposition of ashes on Ash Wednesday, or the offering in a congregation accompanied by music and dance. We connect with something larger than ourselves in these moments and find peace, joy, and purpose.

When a white person visits the Underground Railroad Museum in Cincinnati, Ohio, as part of a church-sponsored pilgrimage (which many congregations did as part of Formative Power), the person enters an experience of disorientation and unease (yes, an example of liminal space noted above). This is because they are stepping outside their comfort zone and into a place of uncertainty. However, this can also be an excellent opportunity for experiences of transcendence as it invites people to let go of old ways of thinking, opening themselves up to new interpretations—many experience transformation, a change in form, a new being.

Just as Paul Tillich wrote about one's ultimate concerns, he wrote about "a new being."[20] Tillich believed that a new being is possible through faith in God. He argued that faith is the act of accepting our ultimate concern, even in the face of anxiety—a white person's realization that racism is an individual and systemic sin. When you and I have faith, we are able to overcome our anxiety, think rather than exclusively feel, experience a change in mind and thus a new way of being. Congregants swim a river path, coming across stronger than the resignation of learning to live with what we can't rise above (to paraphrase Bruce Springsteen's song "Tunnel of Love").[21]

WITH AUTHORITY

As part of the formative project, members of the New Era congregation also visited the National Underground Railroad Freedom Center in Cincinnati just as Common Ground members did.

While on the trip, an older adult stood outside the museum with Dr. Moore, and they both looked across at the bridge known as the John A. Roebling Suspension Bridge. Understand that the Ohio River between Covington and Cincinnati was a possible route for the Confederates to threaten Cincinnati. Furthermore, the member knew the space between the two towns as a river path away from slavery, the enslaved seeking to outrace or swim ahead of the Confederate troops.

She said, "So many people were so close to freedom yet couldn't get across the river. Some drowned; there was no bridge. So many ancestors with no pathway."

She continued, "Now we have to be that bridge."

Dr. Moore later reflected that the Black Church lives in an ocean of fear.

However, Dr. Moore not only leads a Black Church but also addresses the fear associated with racism through powerful worship and the creative power of storytelling with authority.

CONGREGATIONAL ACTIVITY: WORSHIP AND TESTIMONY

What was the nature of Dr. Moore's call?

He remembers, "Some people had more confidence in me than I did in myself. I've always been a storyteller. I have a voice for storytelling."

Dr. Moore's storytelling gift was an early developmental sign of the trail markers competence and authority.

Dr. Moore told stories to neighborhood kids. One story he told was about the ant that lived in the ocean, and the ant didn't drown. He reflects that maybe this is how God was preparing him to preach.

Metaphors are not accidents. Note the phrase "didn't drown" in juxtaposition to the narrative about the enslaved trying to swim across the Ohio River.

Forming People of Racial Reconciliation

Hence, Dr. Moore's storytelling gifts became a congregational activity influencing the positive faith and human development of the New Era congregants.

Now, over time, the two congregations—Common Ground and New Era—have worshipped together three times (and counting).

So, for the sake of immediacy, let's say I (Tim) am a member of Common Ground invited to worship at New Era Church. Let's say you greet me at the front door. Soon worship begins. After brief introductions, Dr. Moore says he'd like to start worship with a story. This is the story we hear:

> Brother Joe was, quote unquote, a free slave. He was free but not really. This was after the Emancipation Proclamation had been given. He was free but not really because Brother Joe couldn't find a job. Brother Joe couldn't really express his freedom in reality. So he fell upon a hard time. But Brother Joe remembered that when he went to church (even though because he was Black he had to sit in the balcony), one of the white parishioners, Miss Susie, always at least said hello to Brother Joe.
>
> Now, Brother Joe thought to himself, "I'm hungry. You know what I'm going to do? I'm going to visit Miss Susie." Brother Joe knocks on the door. Miss Susie peeks through the curtains and she looks to her right and she looks to her left.
>
> She says, "Brother Joe, what are you doing here?"
>
> He says, "Well, Miss Susie, I am hungry, and I need some bread."
>
> Miss Susie looked to her right again and looked to her left.
>
> She said, "Well, Brother Joe, go around to the back door."
>
> Brother Joe went around to the back door. Miss Susie grabbed a loaf of bread and she got ready to give it to Brother Joe.
>
> Now, Miss Susie says, "Before I give you the bread, let's pray."
>
> Brother Joe says, "Okay, Miss Susie."
>
> Miss Susie says, "Our Father." She says, "No, you repeat after me, okay?"
>
> She says, "Our Father."
>
> Brother Joe repeats, he says, "Your Father."
>
> She thinks maybe he didn't understand her. So she says, "Our Father."

He says, "Your Father."

Sister Susie says, "Our Father."

Brother Joe says, "Your Father."

Sister Susie asks, "Now, Joe, how come when I pray 'Our Father' you say, 'Your Father?'"

Brother Joe says, "Miss Susie, if He was our father, that would make me your brother, and you would not ask your brother to go to the back door."

Dr. Moore turns to the congregation(s) and says, "My prayer is that when Common Ground showed up, you got a front-door welcome. Did you all feel that way?"[22]

You, along with a holy host of others, acclaim with confidence, "Amen!" I join in with the vigorous applause that follows.

For a moment, perhaps longer, the distance between the two congregations doesn't seem so far.

The sanctuary is so full of mutual affection, it is almost like the two communities are attached. Such is the formative power of congregations.

QUESTIONS FOR REFLECTION

1. When has your church collaborated with another? Was the collaboration transformative? Did it lead to human development that would not have been possible if there had been no collaboration?
2. What social issue or important topic would members of your congregation benefit by learning more about so as to live more justly?

NOTES

1. Essie Kathryn Scott Payne, *Mama and the Hills of Home: My Spiritual Pillars* (Azure Venture Publishing, 2002).

2. Henry Louis Gates Jr., *The Black Church: This Is Our Story, This Is Our Song* (New York: Penguin, 2021).

3. William Barber, *We Are Called to Be a Movement* (New York: Workman Publishing, 2020).

4. James H. Madison, *The Ku Klux Klan in the Heartland* (Bloomington: Indiana University Press, 2020).

5. University of Notre Dame, "The Most Segregated Hour," March 25, 2021, https://sites.nd.edu/jamesbaldwin/2021/03/25/the-most-segregated-hour (accessed September 23, 2023). Various versions of this quote are attributed to Dr. Martin Luther King Jr., James Baldwin, Malcolm X, and others.

6. Lecrae Moore, foreword to *The Color of Compromise: The Truth about the American Church's Complicity in Racism*, by Jemar Tisby (Grand Rapids, MI: Zondervan, 2019), 17.

7. Jemar Tisby, *The Color of Compromise: The Truth about the American Church's Complicity in Racism* (Grand Rapids, MI: Zondervan, 2019), 137.

8. Amy Jill-Levine, *The Difficult Words of Jesus* (Nashville: Abingdon Press, 2021).

9. Clarence C. Moore and Jeff Krajewski, *Shades of Hope* (podcast), https://podcasts.apple.com/us/podcast/shades-of-hope/id1566911716.

10. Kim Scott, *Radical Candor: Be a Kick-Ass Boss without Losing Your Humanity* (New York: St. Martin's, 2017).

11. Edwin H. Friedman, *Generation to Generation: Family Process in Church and Synagogue* (New York: Guilford, 1985).

12. Robert Kegan, *In Over Our Heads: The Mental Demands of Modern Life* (Cambridge, MA: Harvard University Press, 1994).

13. The Legacy Museum and the National Memorial for Peace and Justice are located on a site in Montgomery, Alabama, where Black people were forced to labor in bondage. It is also just a few blocks away from a rail station where tens of thousands of Black people were trafficked during the nineteenth century. Learn more: https://museumandmemorial.eji.org.

14. Friedman, *Generation to Generation*.

15. *Little Man Tate*, directed by Jodie Foster (Orion Pictures, 1991), DVD.

16. Emmanuel Levinas, *Totality and Infinity: An Essay on Exteriority* (Pittsburgh: Duquesne University Press, 1969).

17. Lawndale Christian Community Church, "About Our Lead Pastor," https://lawndalechurch.org/bio.html (accessed September 23, 2023).

18. Wayne Gordon and John M. Perkins, *Making Neighborhoods Whole: A Handbook for Christian Community Development* (Downers Grove, IL: InterVarsity Press, 2013).

19. Kegan, *In Over Our Heads*.

20. Paul Tillich, *The Courage to Be* (New Haven, CT: Yale University Press, 1959).

21. Bruce Springsteen, "Tunnel of Love," recorded 1987, track 7 on *Tunnel of Love*, Columbia Records, cassette tape.

22. Clarence C. Moore and Jeff Krajewski, "Worship as One," New Era Church, April 30, 2023, video, 38:12, https://www.youtube.com/watch?v=-4LVg_MvC0M&t=331s.

Chapter 6

Forming People of Connection

Reverend Julie Pimlott, a chaplain in southern Indiana and an active member of Main Street United Methodist Church in Boonville, Indiana (where her husband, Rev. Greg Pimlott, serves as pastor), has witnessed firsthand the profound impact of the COVID-19 pandemic on her community. She recognizes the deep pain caused by the isolation and loss of human touch experienced during the acute phase of the pandemic.

Rev. Pimlott observes: "Congregants experienced isolation, loneliness, loss, as well as spiritual malaise."

We know that COVID-19 is tragic and fatal. We also know isolation beginning in March 2020 was necessary. We stayed at home. We canceled our flights. Congregations rescheduled mission trips. We tried to memorize instructions about COVID-positive tests, yet they changed weekly. Which is it? Do we stay away from others for five days after we test positive or after the symptoms are gone?

Also, many did not have the option to stay at home. The debates about working at home after the acute phase of COVID-19 were insensitive to others who had no choice but to work on-site or leave their job. The emergency room worker at the hospital didn't have the option to stay home. Neither did many working on highway repair projects. In other words, we experienced isolation in a variety of ways. Some of us were isolated because we had to work from home. Some of us were isolated because we couldn't work at home.

Is the theme of isolation represented in Scripture? Of course it is. Remember that Jesus healed lepers (Matthew 8:1–4, Mark 1:40–45, Luke 5:12–16). Leprosy was not only a physical affliction; it also led to social isolation. Lepers were forced to live on the outskirts of society, and they had to shout "unclean, unclean" whenever they entered a public place (Leviticus 13:45). Such isolation would be like if one of us had a rash from poison ivy and had to cry "unclean" entering Walmart.

Thankfully, the members of Main Street United Methodist Church were not bound by Levitical law. However, like most people in the world, they experienced isolation during the COVID-19 pandemic. In 2020 and much of 2021, the church body did not meet in person. Worshippers participated via video. Other activities were put on hold. Church leaders had difficult decisions to make as to when to open the sanctuary for in-person worship.

For the leaders of Main Street, the shift from remote to in-person gatherings wasn't a snap decision. It involved a lot of careful consideration and prayer. Eventually, the time came to invite the congregation back together, no longer separated by a virus and mediated by glowing screens.

THE LIFE ARENA OF FRIENDSHIPS

To counter the isolating effects of COVID-19, the leaders at Main Street United Methodist Church embarked on a mission to explore the power of friendship. Leaders like Rev. Julie Pimlott recognized person-to-person interactions, like those in a classroom setting, as crucial in fostering human connection.

Main Street hosts several study groups that provide members with opportunities to form secure and long-lasting attachments. One such group is the "Kitchen Class," which originated in 1961 as the "College and Career Class." As the founding members completed their college education, they updated the group's name to the Kitchen Class, aligning it with its location within the church building. Class members have studied Scripture together for several decades and have flourished as friends.[1]

During the pandemic's most acute phase, church members, including the Kitchen Class, were physically separated from each other on Sundays and during other activities. The absence of weekly in-person interactions with friends inevitably creates pain points. The inability to gather with church friends face-to-face signaled unwanted seclusion. It was heartbreaking to know that someone who sang alongside you in choir was now hospitalized and you couldn't visit.

Of course, human isolation is not a new phenomenon. It predates the pandemic and stems from various factors, including the abundance of online connections (in what way are they connections?), the decline of traditional social groups, increased mobility, and escalating political polarization. The detrimental effects of isolation extend beyond social discomfort; they have a profound impact on physical and mental health, exacerbating conditions like depression, anxiety, suicide, and heart disease. COVID-19 is a twenty-first-century version of leprosy.

Recall that I (Tim) served as the pastor of Westminster Presbyterian Church in Xenia, Ohio. I would stand in the narthex after each service, as clergy do in many congregations, to greet people. Most of these interactions were routine. Occasionally exchanges were more than perfunctory. Joe would shake my hand and casually mention, "By the way, I'm having heart surgery in two weeks," or Angela, holding hands with her spouse Gerald, would announce, "We're expecting a baby."

However, most of the time the greetings were simple: "Good morning," "Nice sermon" (whether it was or not), or "How about those Reds?"

Then one morning, church member Beverly approached. She said, "I wish your sermons were longer."

Surprised, I asked, "Why?"

She replied, "Because if your sermons were longer, there would be fewer moments in the week when I feel alone."

Many aspects of life come together in the congregation. We bring our desire to worship God, to pay attention to an infinitely expansive reality. We pray for health, peace, discernment, and many other aspirations. We also carry to worship the burdens of our human struggles, including destructive elements such as addiction, racism, sexism, and more. Worship may occur in a sanctuary, but it is not a hiding place. Even the most outgoing and lively folks among us can feel an ache of loneliness deep down, tucked away behind our common facades.

Rev. Pimlott created a Formative Power team with the intent of rendering the positive spirit of congregating as a remedy to isolation.

Rev. Pimlott says, "We were lonely and really missed each other. So we began to dream up this idea in early 2021 of hosting classes just for fun, allowing our congregation to come together and renew the relationships that had become distant."

So, brainstorming topics and ultimately implementing the classes began. The team behind the initiative, now called the "Learn-Go-Do Project,"[2] distributed a survey to ask members what they would like to study, and the survey responses guided the team's selection of class topics.

Using the survey results, the team went about choosing the classes they would host. Moving forward, the Main Street United Methodist creators of Learn-Go-Do sought professionals to lead classes, ones who worked in a skilled occupation that required specialized knowledge or training.

The classes offered included:

- Cook Like a Chef
- History of Race through American Film
- Chalk Furniture Painting
- All Kinds of Pie
- Many Ways to Pray
- Watercolor Painting

The Learn-Go-Do Project resonated with congregants by aligning with their interests, perhaps their ultimate concerns, and providing the opportunity for them to direct their own learning journey while enjoying the company of both longtime and new friends. This approach motivated individuals of all ages.

Adults are motivated to learn when the material is relevant to their interests. So, because attendees participated in choosing topics for the Learn-Go-Do Project, they were more likely to engage.

Furthermore, children are naturally curious and eager to learn, and their interests should also be considered when designing educational experiences. Children learn well through hands-on activities. Learning by doing actively engages children instead of passively conveying information. Such play, if you will, makes learning more memorable. An example of this was the popular pie-making class.

MAKING PIES

During Learn-Go-Do, people who did not know each other well became friends, or at least better known to one another. A delightful connection developed between an eight-year-old and an eighty-year-old in the pie-making class. Such a meaningful and intergenerational relationship might never have formed if the older adult's primary link to the church was through operational activities like serving on the council. While they may not have been literally breaking bread together in Emmaus, they did share the experience of making pie in Boonville, Indiana. The prior sentence is not meant to be humorous or a stretch of the truth.

The act of baking may seem like a secular endeavor, yet it indeed takes on a deeper significance when viewed through the lens of faith. For those who believe that Christ's presence can be found in the ordinary moments of everyday life, pie making becomes the starting point for, say, a meaningful friendship, even if it doesn't involve overt spiritual practices like communion or baptism.

The binary view of the sacred and secular, which assigns certain experiences to the realm of the holy while relegating others to the realm of the mundane, fails to capture the essence of human experience. At Main Street, pie making served as a powerful reminder that the sacred is not confined to places of worship or rites of passage; it can permeate every aspect of life, even the seemingly ordinary act of creating a pie.

Here, take and eat.

Main Street's learning activities were supported by a hardy theology, one that linked learning with relationships. Learning strengthened human connection at the expense of isolation.

God exists between people. God assumes such space, signaling that Divine activity exists in the relationships we have with others. God exists between people, not as a distant deity hovering above, but as an in-the-moment presence.

Of course, relationships are not always easy. There will be times of conflict. But it is precisely in these moments of challenge that our awareness of God's presence is most needed—even if we are not aware of our need.

So, acknowledging God's presence in the space between people illustrates God's closeness. In *Life Together*, Dietrich Bonhoeffer wrote, "Friendship is not just a matter of individual affection, but a bond that is rooted in our common life in Christ. It is a gift from God, and it is a gift that we can share with others. Friends are people who love us as we are, and who help us to grow in our love for God and for others.[3]

The Lutheran feminist theologian Dr. Deanna Thompson writes, "God's atoning work for us on the cross is done through Jesus's befriending humanity."[4]

Friendship as atonement is a high-order contrast to substitutionary atonement theology. Sacrificial atonement denotes that Christ died on the cross as a surrogate for sinners; a premium sacrifice, Christ takes on the retaliation we deserve.

An alternative atonement theology is sown with friendship and justice. Atonement is not appeasing an angry God but mending broken relationships to participate in an ever-becoming, more just world. True atonement is represented by closeness and reconciliation with both strangers and friends.

A congregation exploring the life arena of friendship might well explore the emotional, relational aspect of friendship as theology. God is near, and God is a friend—not in a sentimental sense, but in the actuality that God profoundly knows humanity via day-to-day connections.

So, at first glance, the theme of friendship may appear limited in scope, not addressing more significant societal concerns. However, the leaders at Main Street posed a fundamental question: "What could be more important than contending with isolation?" After all, isolation has tangible connections to both physical and mental health issues, contributes to social unrest, and brings about feelings of loneliness. It's no wonder that Main Street prioritized friendship as the foundation for its community-building efforts.

Friendship is a form of soul craft because it has the ability to shape, nurture, and transform our souls. Friendships are typically reciprocal, inviting us to invest our time, energy, and care into the relationships that matter most, our ultimate concerns. Through mutual connection, we are formative energy for the lives of our friends just as we experience formative power for our souls coming from others.

While other organizations and settings, such as schools, neighborhoods, and clubs, provide avenues for friendship formation, Main Street United Methodist Church cultivated a unique environment for fostering friendships within a religious context. They achieved this by embracing a distinctive perspective on God that views one's relationships with others as fractals, miniature reflections of their relationship with the Divine. This perspective emphasizes that meaningful connections with others stem from shared interests, fostering a sense of community and belonging.

A crucial condition for fostering friendships is the presence of a "third thing," a shared interest. A third thing means that in addition to the interactions between people, there is another point of focus, whether it's God or an activity symbolizing the world created by God. Secure adult attachments form around shared activities. The leaders at Main Street recognized the inherent value of this concept, which is why they structured their small-group activities not just for people to share their feelings (which is important) but around shared activities such as painting, pie making, and prayer.

In the context of church, shared activities that hold significance serve as the recipe that seals friendships. Once people embark on a mission trip together, prepare meals for a community dinner, or simply watch a movie side by side, their relationships tend to evolve naturally into solid-state connections even if the particular experience is an exception. That is, we make friends by sharing a third thing, an interest, an activity, and then the friendship grows so that there is less need for an intermediary experience. A leader of Main Street remarked, "We began Learn-Go-Do thinking when we were designing education events, and then we discovered it was friendships that were being designed."

In a Learn-Go-Do class on prayer (the subject of prayer was the third thing), a daughter brought her older-adult father. One of the participants was a young woman in her twenties who had been cautious about engaging in church activities. She usually sat alone during worship services. However, something changed after the prayer class.

The woman in her twenties started sitting with the daughter and her father during worship. The father was showing early signs of dementia, but as their connection grew stronger, he felt more comfortable not hiding his struggles. Similarly, the woman in her twenties now had the chance to break out of her isolation and show her gift for caring, a side of her personality hidden when she sat alone.

The class they shared became the catalyst for their developing relationship, and the connection extended beyond the class.

This vignette provides a transition to trail markers that were not only developing among the three friends noted above, but through almost all of Main Street's formative endeavors.

FIVE TRAIL MARKERS

At least five trail markers represent human development made possible by friendship, trail markers that were strengthened by the education experiences hosted by Main Street.

First, congregations that explore friendship help adherents develop the trail marker of self-differentiation. The space between friends represents God's presence and holy connection, as well as our differences. It is a space where we can be ourselves, even though we, all of us, are unique and therefore different from one another, in ways both subtle and conspicuously overt. There is space for you to be you and for me to be me. A quiet, reserved person can still be naturally quiet and reserved, and such a temperament does not have to have isolation as a consequence. Congregations that offer members opportunities to practice friendship within the assembly can help them develop healthy friendships beyond the congregation with neighbors, acquaintances, and those with differing ideas. Disagreement without maintaining a relationship acts against the Gospel arc of loving both neighbor and stranger. Such a dynamic ultimately leads us to be in relationships with only those like us or who agree with us. Such isolation becomes a non-virus epidemic.

Friendship, as a life arena, draws attention to a second trail marker: attachment. While John Bowlby's attachment theory initially explored the bond between primary caregivers and infants and children, attachment also encompasses our ability to form secure relationships with others throughout our life span. In past generations, congregations served as attachment incubators when assemblies represented an ethnic group (say, Italian Catholics) or neighbors (farming communities), or as places where doctrines were fully accepted by adherents as ultimate truth. Congregations convened within these categories. Congregations functioned as extended families, a natural environment for developing secure attachments. Even without explicit programs focused on friendship, secure connections existed among church members; adult attachment rose as if from the sanctuary's baptismal water. In the United States, the religion of identity existed before identity politics. Geography and particularly European ethnicity no longer solely define congregational belonging. Instead, faith communities foster connections built on shared experiences, values, and a commitment to activities like Bible study, mission trips, and worship. These activities nurture trust and emotional availability among members.

At Main Street United Methodist Church, you will find that a third trail marker is evident: competence. Many of the learning experiences offered involved learning a new skill. I mean competence as the ability, knowledge, or skill to proficiently perform a specific task, job, or function. As a preview, later in this chapter you will read how participants in various educational events learned watercolor painting, chalk furniture painting, and more. If you are part of a pie-making class, you indeed learn about crust, filling, seasoning, pastry mixing, and more. Think of it: your congregation can be your workshop for life skills, including the fun that comes from mastering a perfect pie crust or waving a watercolor brush.

A fourth trail marker also unfolds in the formative experience at Main Street: self-regulation. Remember that emotional regulation results by being the leader of your emotions. Self-regulation is about being able to feel your emotions, whether they're good or bad, without letting them control you. You can name your emotions, express them in healthy ways, and take actions based on them without getting all worked up.

Emotional regulation also means being able to understand and handle the emotions of others. You can listen to people without getting swept away by their feelings, and you can even be influenced by their perspectives while maintaining your own emotional compass.

Instead of reacting impulsively when things get emotional, emotional regulation gives you the agility to pause, listen, share your own thoughts, and even learn something new. I imagine this dynamic has been part of the Kitchen Class experience for years.

Finally, the trail marker integration is part of the experience and development of participants in the Formative course The History of Race in American Film. In psychology, integration refers to merging the different parts of your personality into a cohesive whole. This means accepting both your good and bad qualities, past experiences (both positive and negative), and the full range of emotions you feel. By acknowledging these contrasting aspects, you develop a more complete picture of yourself. This self-awareness allows you to handle challenging realities with more strength. Not only can you accept them, but you can also use them as opportunities to grow and improve.

Imagine this: I'm (Tim) traveling with friends—and we are enjoying being together—to a historical site of the Underground Railroad, a network of secret routes and safe houses that enslaved people used to escape to freedom. Afterwards we grab lunch at Pizza Hut, enjoying the free flow of our conversations. Yet, beneath the surface, we're still processing the weight of learning about this dangerous journey toward liberation. On one hand, I have friends who are the world to me. On the other hand, I can't escape the knowledge that this railroad wouldn't have existed if people like me hadn't exploited others for economic gain.

My messy internal processing represents the developmental dynamic called integration.

All five of these trail markers—self-differentiation, attachment, competence, emotional regulation, and integration—come together in the congregational activity of learning linked with the life arena of friendships. Note that I've identified five trail markers. The high number of trail markers that are part of Main Street's Learn-Go-Do formative experience signals the robust nature of their formative endeavors. The multiple trail markers also indicate that the congregational practice of education and the life arena of friendship are ingredients that abundantly support human development in a religious assembly.

EVEN JESUS NEEDS FRIENDS

Certainly we can hold a robust theology of friendship. How is such a theology traced, even if nuanced, in Scripture? Yes, we are instructed to love our friends and enemies in the Gospels. Both, when you think about it, are hard work. In the book of Acts, we read how Jewish and Gentile people come to terms with their differences, moved to at least the possibility of friendship.

Yet, let's make a move of imagination. We have established that friendship between people is holy space. What about Jesus? How does Jesus, who (theologically) occupies the space between us and another, experience friendship? We have a friend in Jesus. Does Jesus need a friend?

Recall what Jesus conveyed in John 15:15: "I do not call you servants any longer, because the servant does not know what the master is doing, but I have called you friends, because I have made known to you everything that I have heard from my Father."

In chapter 5, I noted the difficult rendering of *doulos* in John 20 as "servant" (sometimes even as "slave"). In this John 15 verse, it appears again. Yet here I want to attend to the word "friend." The Bible Greek word for "friend" as used in John 15:15 is *philos.* It is a common word in the Greek language, and it can be used to refer to a variety of relationships, from casual acquaintances to close companions.

Often the passage is interpreted as a (perhaps awkward) promotion of the disciples from servants to friends. Jesus's trust in his companions has grown. They are no longer Peter, James, John, and the other clueless, stumbling followers sharing Jesus's mission in a frustratingly failing way. No, now they are friends.

Yet what if it isn't so much that Jesus was recognizing the growth of the disciples from clumsy peasants to companions? What if Jesus's pronouncement was because he was lonely? What if it is that Jesus needs friends, not to carry out God's aims but because he needs to experience the intrinsic value of being known by others? After all, being God's favorite child (God loves you best!) isn't the easiest existence.

Jesus's isolation led to a need to be friends with his disciples. He breaks cultural constructs, for example, with the leper as an outsider. Now Jesus has a friend in one who has to shout "unclean" in the public square. Doing so has its costs. People with power dismiss him. Being rejected is not a good feeling. It denotes that something is wrong with you; in this case, the you is Jesus. No one joins Jesus in the house of Pilate at the rigged moment of judgment.

This Jesus needs a friend. He doesn't need servants or disciples; he needs a friend—a person-to-person companionship.

The Christian practice of friendship does not begin with our neediness for friendship to burden Jesus of Nazareth. The practice of friendship begins with our ability to make friends person to person, not just abstractly, with the one, or the One, who is asking you if you will be a friend. The congregation's formative power regarding friendship begins with teaching us to be friends with those who are unfairly isolated from others.

The congregation's formative power of friendship is represented by this odd interpretation that it is Jesus who needs a friend. The congregation carries sacred texts that turn the direction of who saves whom. Additionally, a congregation that provides education about life, about your preferred life activities, activities that may seem mundane yet may be an authentic ground of being for you, provides congregational leaders with welcome relief from having the most important leadership act be choosing the landscaping project for the year or whether or not to buy iPads for the staff (for heaven's sake, they already have laptops!). Certainly, someone must pay attention to institutional maintenance. Yet congregations that prioritize growing in the *life* of faith will intrinsically be healthier institutions. Paying attention to life—your friendships, for example—is institutional maintenance.

In fact, essential to befriending Jesus is paying attention to his life and values, not what has become the culturally conformed church. Jesus is lonely. He wants friends, not more rules about which flowers can be planted on the church grounds.

Now, congregational activities form faith at least as much as if not more than faith forms congregational activities. Christian practices (like friendship) form faith at least as much as if not more than faith forms practice. Furthermore, congregational activities and Christian practice furnish a habitat for God. In fact, participation in Christian practices informed by congregational activities provides sightings of Christ.

Marianne Sawicki maintains this reality in her book *Seeing the Lord*. Sawicki asserts that Gospel texts ("I have called you friends") are not so much testimonies about Christ as they are memories that tell how to see Christ, and, I will add, how to see Christ in the space between you and me. Particular conditions help us access the presence of Jesus Christ. Jesus is not found among the dead. Jesus is found among the living, among people who are doing activities like experiencing acquaintances as friends, listening to people talk about their vocations, even making pies together (who is to say that this can't be an Emmaus road experience?). As Sawicki says, Christ's presence doesn't happen to persons; it happens between and among them.[5]

Yes, Learn-Go-Do was a congregational activity, yet also more than that. Learn-Go-Do embodied the concept of incarnation, where

God takes on human form as Jesus Christ and we are friends with one another just as we befriend the revealing of God in Jesus Christ.

FORMATIVE POWER IS OVERDETERMINED

Main Street United Methodist Church's formative project involved three formative components:

- friendship as the life arena;
- strengthening the trail markers of self-differentiation, attachment, competence, and emotional regulation in adherents; and
- various congregational activities, particularly including educational events and field trips, what I (Tim) like to call pilgrimages.

Just like a pie recipe with many ingredients, there are many contributing factors to human development in congregations.

These "ingredients" include congregational activities, the specific context or life arena, and theological reflection (and it is okay to play with the recipe).

Theological reflection is like adding a special twist—it involves meditating on human development through a theological framework with implications for shaping people's lives.

The source of outcomes is difficult to measure because of the plentitudes of how a congregation forms any one of us to be the person we are. You have multiple ingredients. All occur in different combinations: more sugar, less fruit, and a dash of cinnamon. Formation occurs in unique ways (no two pies are alike). And the beauty is that even throwing in a dash of something unexpected (adjacent activities) can lead to delicious surprises (positive, unforeseen results).

For example, Julie Pimlott describes the power of eating together and the congregational activity of breaking bread with one another. Main Street Church provided a meal every time the Learn-Go-Do events took place. The Learn-Go-Do team did not want the meals to require a lot of volunteers to make, so Julie was willing to be the lead host. Everyone was invited to the meals, regardless of whether they planned to attend the classes afterward or not. Entire households joined in, some staying for the classes and others heading home to attend to homework, chores, and other matters.

By making the invitation available to everyone in the congregation and withdrawing the expectation that attendees had to stay for the classes, Main Street Church was practicing modest open commensality, a term John Dominic Crossan uses as central to Jesus's ethic.[6] Open commensality refers to the practice of sharing meals together without social barriers or hierarchies. It's about creating a space where everyone, regardless of background or status, eats together as equals.

In the parable of the wedding banquet (Matthew 22:1–14), Jesus compares the kingdom of heaven to a lavish feast that a king prepares for his son's wedding. He invites many guests, but those initially invited refuse (not recommended). The king sends servants to invite them again, but the response is not welcomed, and some servants are even mistreated and killed.

So the king decides to open the invitation to anyone willing to come. There is more, however. A person shows up at the banquet wearing clothes that do not meet the dress code, and Jesus casts the person out. This act of inhospitality is not consistent with Jesus's ethic and is considered by some to be a later addition to the manuscript.[7]

Regardless, by providing meals for everyone, regardless of whether they planned to attend the classes afterward, Main Street Church was practicing a fine miniature of Jesus's open invitation represented in the parable. The meals were formative activities that reinforced friendship and hospitality.

MOVIES AS CONGREGATIONAL PRACTICE

But wait, there's more. Amid pie making and finger painting, another Learn-Go-Do class was offered, a class briefly alluded to above: The History of Race through American Film taught by Dr. Betty Hart, a retired professor at the University of Southern Indiana.

One of the movies represented a congregational practice essential to the development of those linked to Main Street: the movie *Harriet*.[8]

The film follows Harriet Tubman's journey from slavery in the Deep South to freedom in Philadelphia, where she helped dozens of enslaved people escape to the North. It also explores her relationship with the antislavery activists she worked with, many of whom were inspired by her determination and intimidated by her fierceness.

Like many films about historical figures, some aspects of the character and events are changed or simplified for the audience's sake. However, the film received excellent reviews and is generally considered a faithful and accurate portrayal of Harriet Tubman's life.[9]

In one historically accurate scene, Harriet Tubman (then known as Araminta, or Minty) stands on a bridge above rushing water while being chased by the man who claimed ownership over her. She looks at the torrent beneath, then back to the danger behind her. Minty exclaims, "Live free or die!" She bravely jumps from the bridge into the rushing water and ultimately swims to freedom.[10]

The congregational practice known as testimony is an important part of human development, particularly the developmental trail marker called integration, a concept discussed in chapter 4. In this specific context, Harriet Tubman's testimony, as portrayed in the film, offers an opportunity for the class to navigate the complex landscape of their desires to be allied with those who were enslaved in the past, those currently living under such conditions, and those who will face such oppression in the future. Additionally, Harriet Tubman's testimony, as represented by the film, invited (maybe forced) class members to confront their complicity, whether implicit or explicit, in benefiting from the systemic structures that perpetuate oppression.

One participant noted, "I joined the group because I wanted to get to know a particular person better who was also part of the class, and I did. I am also glad I learned more about the history of race in this country. I lived through some of the history we talked about (another movie the group watched was *Selma*[11]). We have come a long way in terms of race, but we still have a long way to go."

GOING UNDERGROUND

Remember that the Main Street Church is in Boonville, Indiana, in Warrick County, southern Indiana.

Boonville is a fine town, small, with a population under seven thousand. It bears the name of Senator Ratliff Boon. The current post office is the home of a large mural called *Boonville Beginnings*, a New Deal artwork, as in Franklin Roosevelt and the New Deal. The old Warrick County Jail is on the National Register of Historic Places.

Developing ideas about the "go" part of the formative experience was challenging. Members of Main Street are frugal and humble. So, early in the formative process, the formative team asked members to dream about what they might want to do and where they would want to go. The first round of ideas that emerged were good but commonplace. For example, the members traveled to the neighboring city of Evansville for lunch.

Yes, human development and faith formation may occur through modest activities in incremental ways. However, the formative process provided resources for congregations to dream, to think expansively.

Modest is good. Yet, as congregants, we change and grow as human beings when we travel to the edge of what is known to us, including when we experience life together beyond committee meetings and recruiting volunteers to clean the church basement. Occasionally we need to dislocate to learn.

As noted in chapter 5, a common theme regarding human development is that liminal experiences signify a crucial role in human development. Recall that liminal experience is a feeling of disorientation during an in-between phase, on the verge of something new. Such experiences send us into the great wide open, a sense that life holds much more than we know, even if the much more isn't at first clear. This is life at a threshold.

However, threshold experiences can also be troubling. Sometimes the uncertainty is so disturbing that we withdraw inside ourselves. Through the formative process, we received feedback from congregational leaders that while liminal experiences resulted in growth, such experiences also require a sense of emotional safety for new insights and behaviors to be sustained. Without this crucial support, this threshold phase can devolve into a paralyzing state where our capacity for learning gives way to the primal need for security.

The essential safety zone is often provided by connection with others. The leaders at Main Street realized early on that educational events were catalysts for friendships and, alternatively, friendships strengthened learning experiences. Friendships are not only a source of happiness and support but also a powerful tool for learning and growth. In their book *The Power of Moments*, Chip and Dan Heath explore the science of how to create memorable and meaningful experiences. The authors argue that one of the most important factors in creating these experiences is to share them with others. They found that shared experiences are more likely to be remembered and to have a lasting impact on our lives. We are better communal learners than solo learners.[12]

With encouragement from the formative team to think big and imaginatively about the formative process, church members committed to traveling to the National Underground Railroad Museum in Cincinnati (just as members of New Era Church and Common Ground Church did, as described in chapter 5).

The trip to the Cincinnati museum was a developmental next step produced naturally by the History of Race through American Film class.

A particularly impactful exhibit at the museum for Main Street members was the Slave Pen.[13] This exhibit of an actual pen, likely built in the early 1800s, served as a stark reminder of the sin of slavery. During this era, slave pens were used to hold and transport enslaved individuals before selling them or to move them to other locations for forced labor. These damp, dark, and unsanitary holding cells were places of immense trauma and isolation.[14]

Imagine a member of the Main Street Church standing in front of this slave pen. She might be thinking, "How could this ever have happened?"

Such a question represents a breach in our emotional center. The phrase "emotional center" refers to the core of our sentient being. It is where our sense of self and our beliefs are stored. Shaken emotional centers challenge core beliefs. This is disorienting. It tosses us into a state of liminality. The familiar crumbles. We grapple to find new ground.

So, yes, navigating such shaky terrain requires support. Our trust in others calms our emotional center as if an angel is speaking, "Do not be afraid." We remain open and vulnerable enough to ask the critical question: "How could this ever have happened?"

Picture driving before the days of Google Maps and arriving at an unfamiliar crossroad, say a seldom-traveled road in southern Indiana. You are unsure of the way forward, yet you must make a choice: continue the same path, turn left, or turn right. Similarly, confronting sins of the past demands a choice: to ignore, to turn away, or, however hesitantly, to accept the discomfort and vulnerability necessary for growth.

After their trip to the National Underground Railroad Museum, the Main Street travelers cruised south for an hour. They arrived in Milton, Kentucky, at a bed-and-breakfast called Richwood on the River. There they learned that the establishment's name had only been recently changed from Richwood Plantation when new management arrived. While at Richwood on the River, the travelers heard the story of an enslaved person fleeing the plantation and swimming across the river to Madison on a barrel or a raft made of scrap wood.

A plantation, of course, isn't just any farm, at least not a *slave* plantation. A slave plantation was a large farm that used enslaved people to grow and harvest crops. Now we may refer to family farms, and with such farms comes a positive or nostalgic sensation. Not so for plantations of the enslaved. A slave plantation was a landscape corrupted for the purpose of imprisonment, the worst possible jail.

While at the plantation home, church members had access to the whole house. The owner was gone, and there were no other guests.

They went downstairs to the basement. The basement visit required that the church be its own tour guide. There was no one to show them around.

As they stood in the dimly lit basement, imagination led to curiosity. What if this wasn't the basement of a comfortable bed-and-breakfast in 2022? Could this be a portal to the nineteenth century, a time hidden in many official history textbooks?

If it were the nineteenth century, the visitors would be standing in a contested space. Madison, Indiana, is situated across the Ohio River from Kentucky, a slave state. This strategic positioning made it a crucial hub for the Underground Railroad, a secret network of safe houses and routes that helped refugee enslaved people escape to freedom. So, though the farm used the enslaved for labor, it was possible that the house, that is, the basement, was a holding environment for the enslaved seeking freedom. The lore about this particular plantation is that one of the family members might have been passively allowing the basement to be used in this way (while still using the enslaved to plant and harvest crops), a nineteenth-century "don't ask, don't tell" situation.

So, now, imagine the church members in the basement. Without the pleasure of a tour guide, the members used their imagination and constructed a story unimpeded by disputed facts.

What was it like to be on the run, hiding alone in the basement?
What was it like to be alone in the basement, knowing others were in the field?
Was this basement a slave pen or a safe house?
Was the basement unsanitary?
I wonder if the owner ever went down to the basement.
Who can tell the accurate, truthful history of this home?

It was as if the Main Street members were producing their own movie about the history of race in the United States.

Before the pilgrims of Main Street returned to their rooms for sleep, they gathered for evening prayer. The evening devotion included lighting a candle, a hymn, a prayer, a Scripture reading, and silent reflection (a form of prayer, silent prayer). The Scripture reading was Galatians 3:27–29:

> As many of you as were baptized into Christ have clothed yourselves with Christ. There is neither Jew nor Greek, there is no longer slave or free, there is no longer male and female, for all of you are one in Christ Jesus. And if you belong to Christ, then you are Abraham's offspring, heirs according to the promise.

In one of the Learn-Go-Do classes, the topic of prayer was explored using the resource *7 Ways to Pray* by Amy Boucher Pye. Although the curriculum for the two classes 7 Ways to Pray and A History of Race in America may have been different, the entire church community was collectively grasping the profound connection between justice and prayer.

I (Tim) believe that if a specific group within the church delves into a learning experience that others might not be directly engaged in, the entire church body still benefits through God's synchronicity. In any case, Amy Boucher Pye proposes that:

> [God] receives our longings and our praise, our petitions and our thanks. . . . Not only does [God] respond to the cries of our hearts and the offhand prayers we utter, but [God] changes us . . . through the working of the Holy Spirit in our lives . . . we become more compassionate and caring, more self-controlled and outward looking, wiser and with greater understanding.[15]

The Main Street travelers had one more stop. They went to the site of Eleutherian College in Lancaster, Indiana, a college created by anti-slavery Baptists. The word "eleutherian" comes from the Greek word *eleutheros*, meaning freedom and equality. This Greek word is used ten times in the New Testament, including in 2 Corinthians 3:17: "Now the Lord is the Spirit, and where the Spirit of the Lord is, there is freedom."

The school admitted students regardless of ethnicity or gender, including freed and fugitive enslaved human beings beginning in 1847. The school was the second college in the United States west of the Allegheny Mountains and the first in Indiana to provide education to students of different colors. Eleutherian College began offering university-level classes in 1848.

The chapel is the whole first floor, complete with six two-story windows and a balcony above the two entrances to the room from the foyer. The Main Street Church members saw the signatures of hundreds of students written on old plaster walls, students who made their mark two hundred years ago.

Just as in Christina's family, my family (Tim's) have annually measured and marked the height of each person in our household. We then signed our respective names next to the measurements. We will leave those numbers and signatures until a Realtor tells us to paint them over when we sell the home. Signatures are not only for legal documents. Signatures also express who you are, representing your personality, style, and the image you wish to project. The way you sign your name conveys individuality and creativity, a variation on *eleutheros*. Students who passed through Eleutherian College added their signatures, a symbolic expression of the freedom they experienced in this transformative place.

The signatures also signified the relationships that existed way back when, and to this day through those that bear witness.

Sometimes we learn the hard way. Yet we learn, change, grow, and act consistently with our most just values through connection with others. We don't have to face the cellar of discomfort alone. Connection is fertile ground. When we navigate difficult times with others, we are less likely to deny uncomfortable truths. Even if we find ourselves in the depths of discomfort, the simple act of being with others, or even the memory of past support, can shift our emotional core toward resilience.

There are those who say that we grow through hard times and that times of great suffering are our best teachers. I don't believe this is true, at least not completely true. We develop in spite of suffering. The deeper reality is that suffering produces development when we are connected to a cloud of witnesses. Human development's greatest allies are securely attached relationships. We develop through suffering, despite the suffering, when we are held by others.

When the Main Street travelers returned to their Boonville church building, each got out of the car they had been traveling in. One member said, "This was one of the most important things I've done my whole life."

FORMATIVE IMPACT

The Formative Power framework for congregations asserts that congregational life does change people and that congregational participation can result in positive physical, psychological, emotional, and social changes for individuals and, indeed, for communities of faith and perhaps the larger community.

Furthermore, we wager that participation in a congregation nourishes growth in one's relationship with God and one's developmental capacity related to an ultimate concern. While some congregations prioritize character development and growth in faith, others may not view faith as a progressive endeavor. Some individuals may outgrow their congregation's capacity to nurture their faith, while others question the validity of measuring faith development.

Nevertheless, we are changed by participation in congregational life. Womanist theology (described more fully in chapter 1) starts with the experience of Black women rather than esoteric ideas. Planted by the experience of Black women, womanist theology naturally informs a contextual practical theology that draws on the real-life struggles and joys of congregations. Womanist theology, as an expression of a particular context at a particular time, respectfully holds and accepts congregants' lived experiences, and adherents then define their own truths. "This is one of the most important things I've done my whole life." Such a comment signifies growth, developmental growth.

Yet, if growth is desired, how is it measured? Is there an inventory that could or should be developed? Or can faith and human development in a congregation be documented through anecdotes and stories? Is it possible, or should it be possible, to evaluate the faith capacity and the human development of not only individuals but the church as a whole body, the body of Christ?

Some congregations have found thinking in terms of results and impact helpful.

Results are the immediate and short-term outcomes of a program or intervention. Impact is the longer-term and broader effects of such programs.

Results are typically measured in terms of specific outputs or outcomes, such as the number of people who participated in a program. Therefore, a result would be the number of people who attended the showing of the movie *Harriet*.

Impact is typically measured in terms of changes in behavior, attitudes, or knowledge that can be attributed to the program.

The Main Street member's reflection on the movie *Harriet* ("We have come a long way in terms of race, but we still have a long way to go") captures the ongoing developmental inertia of learning, experiencing, and doing.

IMPACT QUOTES

To close out the year of Learn-Go-Do at Main Street United Methodist Church, Rev. Julie Pimlott invited participants to break bread together once again. She asked them to reflect on their experiences and what participation meant to them. The following reflections represent participants' lived experience and offer a step toward assessing the impact of the congregation's endeavor:

- After spending a year and half looking at our own walls, arguing with people on Facebook about toilet paper and other topics, it was good to have something to come to and be with other people and have fun. Also, the Go-Do trip to the Newfield Museum was a life changer for me. I studied art in college but had never had the

chance to go to a major museum. I got to see a Van Gogh in person, and I just stood in front of it and cried.
- I think, as I grow older, it is important to continue to have activities that you enjoy, because it is good for your physical, mental, and spiritual health. These groups gave me something to look forward to and helped me maintain my health.
- I was relatively new to this congregation, and being in these groups helped me meet people. Susie [not her real name] and I sat together and chatted and painted, and I really enjoyed the whole class.
- I have always enjoyed cooking. Getting to do this class with my brother and sister was great.
- We laughed; we had fun. I always looked forward to being here.
- As a retired person, it is important to keep learning new things and skills, even after you retire. I made some goals to learn things after I retired; some I have met and some not yet. And when I heard about these classes, I thought I should join one and keep learning and growing.

POSTLUDE

Imagine you're a member of Main Street United Methodist Church. You're standing in the bustling hallway while various classes are in full swing. You sense the energy flowing in the classrooms, where animated conversations, laughter, and the movement of people are all in play.

You might have a personal connection to one of the classrooms as you stand there. It could be your child's class or a child you've come to know and care about through shared moments in worship. Your curiosity gets the best of you, and you decide to peek inside this room.

Inside, you spot an adult engaging with a child in a heartfelt conversation. The child wears a bright, enthusiastic smile that says, "Look at what I've accomplished!" You stand at the threshold, positioned between the classroom and the hallway, and in that moment you can't help but feel joy.

You are looking at an iPhone photo moment to be shared, representing people at their best. You are witnessing the embodiment of the church's essence—a place of growth, a community that nurtures friendships, an assembly of people exploring what matters most to them aligned with God's intentions. It's a reminder that within these walls, individuals of all ages actively engage with the trinity of church, life, and personal growth. It's a scene that distills the heart of your church community, where faith and life intersect, fostering continuous development regarding what it means to be a human being at this time and in this place. This continuous unfolding, this precious crossing of the threshold, is the most important thing your church is doing.

QUESTIONS FOR REFLECTION

1. Who were among your first friends in a congregation and what impact have such friendships had on your life?
2. How would you describe the connection between education and friendship?

NOTES

1. Main Street United Methodist Church, "Grow Deeper," https://www.mainstreetumcboonville.com/serve (accessed September 23, 2023).

2. Center for Congregations, "Learn Go Do: A Transformative Journey of Community Engagement," https://centerforcongregations.org/stories/learn-go-do-a-transformative-journey-of-community-engagement-at-main-street-umc (accessed September 23, 2023).

3. Dietrich Bonhoeffer, *Life Together: The Classic Exploration of Christian Community* (New York: HarperCollins, 1954), 55.

4. Deanna A. Thompson, *Crossing the Divide: Luther, Feminism, and the Cross* (Minneapolis: Fortress Press, 2004), 135.

5. Marianne Sawicki, *Seeing the Lord* (Minneapolis: Fortress Press, 1994), 79.

6. John Dominic Crossan, *The Historical Jesus: The Life of a Mediterranean Jewish Peasant* (New York: HarperCollins, 1991), 421–22.

7. Bernard Brandon Scott, *Hear Then the Parable: A Commentary on the Parables of Jesus* (Minneapolis: Fortress Press, 1989), 163.

8. *Harriet*, directed by Kasi Lemmons (Focus Features, 2019), DVD.

9. A. O. Scott, "Harriet Review: Becoming Moses," *New York Times*, October 31, 2019, https://www.nytimes.com/2019/10/31/movies/harriet-review.html (accessed December 7, 2023).

10. *Harriet*.

11. *Selma*, directed by Ava DuVernay (Paramount Pictures, 2014), DVD.

12. Chip Heath and Dan Heath, *The Power of Moments: Why Certain Experiences Have Extraordinary Impact* (New York: Simon & Schuster, 2017).

13. The Slave Pen exhibit at the National Underground Railroad Freedom Center plays an integral role in telling the greater story of the internal slave trade in the United States. The pen was originally built in the early 1800s and was recovered from a farm in Mason County, Kentucky, less than sixty miles from the Freedom Center. The structure was used as a holding pen by Kentucky slave trader Capt. John W. Anderson to temporarily warehouse enslaved people who would be sold farther south. Learn more: https://freedomcenter.org/visit/permanent-exhibits/the-slave-pen.

14. Richwood on the River (formerly Richwood Plantation) in Milton, Kentucky, now serves as a bed-and-breakfast and special event/wedding venue. Built in 1803, it was once a slavery-era plantation. Learn more: https://richwoodontheriver.com.

15. Amy Boucher Pye, *7 Ways to Pray: Time-Tested Ways for Encountering God* (Colorado Springs: NavPress, 2021), 9.

Chapter 7

Forming a Creative Congregation

WHY GROW CREATIVITY?

In a bustling city, a woman feels disconnected and stressed from her corporate job. One evening, she found an old sketchbook and began drawing again, rekindling her childhood passion. Sketching became her evening ritual, bringing her peace and helping her process emotions.

In a small town, a young boy struggles with reading in school despite his best efforts leaving him frustrated and discouraged. One day, his teacher noticed his affinity for drawing and encouraged him to use it to aid his learning. He began to illustrate the stories he read, drawing scenes and characters that brought the words to life and the remarkable happened—his understanding and retention improved, his grades began to rise, and his confidence grew.

In the 1940s, Jacob Lawrence created "The Migration Series," a powerful collection of 60 paintings. This series depicted the mass movement of African Americans from the rural South to the urban North in search of better opportunities and escaping racial oppression. Lawrence's vibrant, narrative style brought to life the struggles and resilience of Black Americans and documented this crucial chapter in American history sparking national conversations about race, migration, and equality.

It is not fully understood in just how many ways creativity is essential for growth. According to one psychologist, creativity can be defined as the ability to come up with original ideas, to put ideas or images or experiences together in new ways.[1] Or, as Albert Einstein once said, it is the ability to see what others see and think what no one else has ever thought. While not completely understood, what we do know is that creativity is often a life force that enlivens, transports, and translates our innermost ideas into the world in remarkable ways.

There have been attempts to measure the impact of creativity on development. For instance, it has been well documented that creativity in the form of arts education such as music, theater, art, and other forms of creative expression improve children's academic, social, and emotional outcomes.[2] While adults at times have limited outlets for creative expression, studies have shown that it remains critical for well-being for creativity to be nurtured and encouraged throughout adulthood.[3] Creativity plays an indispensable role in personal growth across the life span to enable ongoing development of cognitive flexibility, emotional well-being, social competence, and identity exploration. Let's look at each benefit, including cognitive, emotional, relational, and identity development, in greater depth.

Cognition

Creativity helps us develop our thinking abilities. Jean Piaget's famous theory of cognitive development highlights the ways creativity aids in cognitive development, contending that creative thinking emerges from the assimilation and accommodation of new information.[4] It is also understood that engaging in creative activities enhances cognitive flexibility, problem-solving skills, and divergent thinking. This in turn fosters the development of complex cognitive structures and adaptive strategies.[5]

Emotional Regulation

Creativity also aids us in developing emotional regulation. Erick Erikson's psychosocial theory emphasizes the importance of identity formation and emotional regulation throughout the life span. At times, however, it is difficult for persons to understand and process what they are experiencing emotionally. Creative expression provides a conduit for this kind of emotional exploration and catharsis.[6] As individuals engage in creative processes, they confront and process emotions, promoting self-awareness and emotional well-being. In this way, creative activities function as tools for processing social and emotional experiences.

Attachment

How about creativity and how we connect with others? According to attachment theory, secure attachments during early childhood foster healthy social development.[7] Creative play, a hallmark of childhood, promotes social interaction, cooperation, and negotiation. Additionally, group creative endeavors encourage collaboration, empathy, and perspective taking, enhancing the development of prosocial skills essential for successful social interactions.[8]

Identity

For many of us, adolescence is marked by the search for identity. Creativity plays a pivotal role in this quest by providing a means for self-expression, experimentation, and identity exploration.[9] While this can be both a confusing and exciting time for adolescents and their families, adolescents' engagement in creative pursuits, whether artistic or intellectual, facilitates the integration of diverse aspects of the self, contributing to the development of a coherent and authentic identity.

As one can see, creativity's impact on personal development is multifaceted and pervasive. It is also ongoing and transcends age boundaries. In adulthood, creative activities continue to serve as outlets for continued growth, self-expression, and cognitive engagement.[10] Creativity's role in promoting cognitive vitality aligns with theories of successful aging, emphasizing the importance of engagement in stimulating and purposeful activities throughout life. It comes as no surprise, then, that fostering creativity within a multigenerational congregation is a tremendously transformative endeavor.

Chapter 7

WHY FORM A CREATIVE CONGREGATION?

Congregations have long been regarded as sanctuaries of spiritual growth and communal connection. However, the arts, encompassing visual arts, music, dance, theater, and literature, offer unique avenues through which congregational members can engage with their faith, explore their identity, and forge meaningful relationships. The case study in this chapter in many ways explores the symbiotic relationship between the arts, theology, and human development within congregations, shedding light on their catalytic transformative potential. We will explore the many benefits that can be reaped through fostering creative expression within congregations, including being a means of transcendence, connection, theological reflection, embracing diversity, and creating social change.

Transcendence

Congregations are sites of transcendent experience through many available means. Through mediums such as sacred art, music, and rituals, congregational members can experience a profound connection to the faith they espouse. Visual representations of religious narratives, melodic chants, and choreographed dances all serve as conduits for conveying and embodying theological concepts. It is one level of understanding to be able to describe the Word made flesh and another to be able to enflesh the Word through dance, theater, or other embodied expression, transcending what can be conveyed with words alone.

Connection

The arts also play a pivotal role in creating a sense of community within congregations. Choirs, theater groups, and art workshops offer spaces where individuals can collaborate, share their talents, and form strong interpersonal connections. By participating in artistic endeavors collectively, congregational members build a sense of belonging and mutual support. This sense of community enhances both individual and collective well-being, creating a nurturing environment to be seen, known, and mentored in one's craft.

Theological Reflection

In addition to the potential for transcending and connecting, the arts also encourage congregants to grapple with complex theological ideas, fostering intellectual curiosity and theological reflection. Religious iconography, sacred music, and dramatic performances can prompt congregants to contemplate theological truths and ethical dilemmas in novel, nonthreatening ways. The arts offer an alternative mode of engaging with religious teachings beyond verbal processing and invite congregational members to reinterpret and deepen their theological understanding through multiple manners of expression.

Diversity

The arts can be a profound method of promoting inclusivity by allowing diverse voices and perspectives to be expressed in congregational life. Artistic endeavors can serve as platforms for congregational members from various backgrounds to share their stories and traditions. This diversity of expression enriches the congregational experience, fostering a more inclusive and open-minded community that values the uniqueness of each individual. Congregations with the capacity to navigate diversity within their community lead to congregants who are able to navigate diversity between communities.

Social Change

What impact can congregational creativity have in the public square? The arts have very often been sources of social change. From civil to human rights movements, the arts have a uniquely compelling way of bringing attention to that which otherwise goes ignored. One example of how art can highlight social issues took place here in Indianapolis. During the summer of 2020, a colorful mural on the streets of downtown Indianapolis that spelled out #BlackLivesMatter along with an image of a raised fist was painted by eighteen local artists.[11] The mural was painted on Indiana Avenue, the historic hub of the city's Black culture and the original location of Witherspoon Presbyterian Church, which we will hear more about soon. A week after its completion, it was vandalized with gray and white splattered paint, which, according to the artists, was important for the world to see, as it was evidence of the very racism the mural was seeking to address and underscored why such movements matter. Indeed, art can shape social change by shedding light on matters in such a way that even an attempt to cover it can enhance its message all the more.

In both bold public and intimate congregational contexts, the arts transcend mere aesthetic pursuits and harness formative power integral to change. This power includes the capacity to inspire spiritual growth, strengthen community bonds, foster cognitive and emotional development, encourage theological reflection, and embrace diversity, showcasing the transformative power of artistic expression. As congregational leaders and theologians, recognizing and cultivating the role of the arts in shaping human development can lead to more holistic and enriching spiritual journeys for congregants, forging a deeper connection between faith and artistic creativity.

One church we worked with was especially committed to exploring what creativity could do to spur growth in its congregation. The congregation was Witherspoon Presbyterian Church located on the west side of Indianapolis, has a unique history. In 1907, Witherspoon Presbyterian Church became the first Indianapolis church of the denomination to serve the African American community, and it has continued this legacy of courage and innovation ever since.

WHO IS WITHERSPOON PRESBYTERIAN CHURCH?

I enjoyed learning about Witherspoon Presbyterian Church and the formative project they developed just as much as I enjoyed talking with the senior pastor, Rev. Dr. Winterbourne LaPucell Harrison-Jones. I sat down with Pastor Harrison-Jones, a stately, wise, and incredibly humble soul, to get to know this congregation better and the ways that the Formative Power project had shaped them. To its pastor, Witherspoon Presbyterian Church is a vibrant, life-giving, historic congregation in Indianapolis whose story began on the avenue, an epicenter of arts and African American life in the early twentieth century.[12] Pastor Harrison-Jones shared that the congregation then moved to its current location in the 1960s in order to expand their reach to the west side of Indianapolis. As is clear from its origin story, this congregation's niche has always been arts and culture, a church that serves as a convening space for Black creativity with a spiritual epicenter. At the time of our conversation, Pastor Harrison-Jones had been the pastor of this historical congregation for about three years. He spoke of the church's formative story as one that included a good deal of transition and change as they had been on a journey of discerning, reconciliation, and reimagining. From this congregational reimagining, they were poised and ready to move forward into a new season with renewed focus and a reestablished sense of identity and call.

Such community transitions are not unlike developmental stages that individuals traverse. We begin to examine who we are, where we have been, and from there (re)define and envision who we can be in the future. Perhaps this congregational developmental stage has elements of Erick Erikson's psychosocial developmental stage of identity versus role confusion or generativity versus stagnation. Either way, such wrestling can be said to be an expected and healthy expression of growth in individuals and collectives.

For Witherspoon Church, this developmental stage included a creative use of imagery as they developed a new logo with accompanying guiding values. Pastor Harrison-Jones explained that out of the process of honoring a historical legacy and situating themselves as oriented toward the next generation came the program they named the Imani Community Wellness Project. The name Imani was inspired by the last Kwanzaa principle, formulated by Maulana Karenga in 1966.[13] Imani represents the principle of faith, but as Harrison-Jones added, it is also a nod to the other commitments of Kwanzaa that seek to honor the whole person. The whole person for Witherspoon included mind, body, and spirit.

WITHERSPOON'S FORMATIVE PROJECT

Among one of the primary components of the Imani Wellness Project was the Actors Ink program. Actors Ink was an acting company for people aged fifty-five and over. This group met virtually during the COVID-19 pandemic. Pastor Harrison-Jones recalls how much of a developmental task this was since some of these same individuals did not have an email address prior to COVID-19. Nonetheless, as a congregation, they pulled together to get everyone online to create together. He shares that despite the obstacles presented by COVID-19, Actors Ink remained engaged virtually and completed a second season with great success. They were able to produce an original show titled *Got Something to Say* and began making plans for their next season. Meanwhile, he stated, the work with the Asante Art Institute flourished into a series of outdoor performances centered around social justice and civil rights, titled "Journey in Search of Justice." Thanks to the hard work and creativity of both Asante and Witherspoon, the outdoor campus was able to be transformed into an arts amphitheater and attracted over two hundred attendees. The show was so successful it was filmed by WFYI and shown throughout the state, and thanks to a partnership with the IUPUI School of Education, a curriculum has been written and made available to teachers statewide.[14]

The Imani Community Wellness Program not only engaged the Witherspoon congregation but created opportunities to build deeper relationships across generations and push the social consciousness of the congregation. Harrison-Jones described 2020 as a turbulent year, especially concerning race relations in America. The year was laden with pain, bloodshed, and social protests throughout the nation. Harrison-Jones noted that the winds of Pentecost blew throughout the nation and ignited the moral resolve of people who otherwise may never have answered the call to think prophetically and act boldly in the face of injustice. Because of this, Harrison-Jones believes the Witherspoon congregation had to not only respond to the pressing calls for justice with the Black Lives Matter movement, but also to challenge its own congregational stances on other forms of injustice and marginalization. From out of the quagmire of lament, he reflects, a series of social justice conversations emerged from within the congregation that included members and community friends that stretched across every generation. He recalls that the topics were deep and personal, and oftentimes marked by tears.

Finally, after many months of virtual engagement and brainstorming, one of the youngest members of the team said, "We've talked long enough. Let's write it down." And so, Harrison-Jones recounts, over a matter of weeks, two congregational credos were shaped, one in support of Black Lives Matter, and the other, a first in the history of Witherspoon, a statement proclaiming Witherspoon as an open and affirming congregation.[15]

Pastor Harrison-Jones describes the congregation during the time following its Formative Power project as one that, in the words of theologian Howard Thurman, "came alive."[16] One such example included the discovery that there was a member who had been at the church for years who was a seamstress but who was also an acting teacher. Pastor Harrison-Jones described the gifts and talents of so many people emerging as they were given space to "awaken." He basked when considering the intergenerational dynamics, from youth as understudies of technology personnel to elders who were paired with fifth graders to have conversations about injustice. As a result, Pastor Harrison-Jones was awestruck that traffic throughout the sanctuary no longer took place without eye contact. Instead, he could tell that members were known and seen by one another in deeper and more meaningful ways.

By the end of the project, the pastor described the congregation as "yeasty," "effervescent," and "alive." He described such feelings as contagious and palpable to newcomers. He even noticed that there were past members of the church who were finding their way back with curiosity and engagement that, as they shared with him, they had not felt since they were children. In this he rejoiced.

HOW WAS THE PASTOR FORMED?

In closing the conversation with the Pastor of Witherspoon Presbyterian Church, we reflected on how the formative project not only formed the congregation but formed him as a pastor. He said that he feels like a better pastor primarily because the project helped demystify him as the pastor and helped him earn the title of the congregation's shepherd. He gets emotional as he describes the honor it has been to love and care for one another with candor, tenderness, and humanity. He then tells the story of telling a particular member, "I see you," and putting his hand on her shoulder. This member now grabs his hand and says, "I see you, too." What joy, he exclaims!

Pastor Harrison-Jones also notes that he grew from the cohort model of the Formative Power program as well. His particular cohort included about eight different church leaders who dreamed and developed their projects together. He went on to say that they had helped each other by speaking at one another's events and by otherwise being resources for each other. Harrison-Jones said that it was formative to be a part of a team and that he feels transformed as a result.

While there were many examples of positivity generated by Witherspoon's participation in the formative project process, as with all congregations, Harrison-Jones's was greatly impacted by COVID-19. Not the least of the impacts were deaths of church members. In the midst of it all, Harrison-Jones acknowledged that some of what was originally intended to be more of a shared leadership framework for developing and implementing the project became operated primarily through the pastor's office. Rather than being overtaken by

Figure 7.1 Formative Power Framework

these unexpected realities, there was an intentional effort to reshape the project so that it met the original objectives and would not be abandoned. While challenging, Harrison-Jones remarks that the fruit of his labor was sustaining.

CASE STUDY REFLECTIONS

There are so many dimensions of powerful transformation and growth within the story of Witherspoon Presbyterian Church. The intergenerational relationship attachment bonds and artistic and technical competencies built through the Actors Ink program and the growing capacity for difficult conversations that led to establishing new stances on social matters such as Black Lives Matter and becoming an open and affirming congregation stand out most to me. Figure 7.1 presents a visual representation of how these features look within the Formative Power project framework.

Trail Markers

Increased secure attachment was evidenced most clearly through the capacity for members to look at each other eye-to-eye rather than simply passing one another by. But what's more, they tested the security of their attachments by embarking on difficult conversations, coming out on the other side with clarity of mind, purpose, conviction, and identity. Another indicator of attachment growth was that the project was initially going to be in four phases in which participants could cycle in and out. Instead, the leadership was surprised at how many wanted to stay and continue. They had bonded and were not interested in detaching.

Additionally, several competencies were discovered, gained, and developed through acting class, technology proficiency, and a variety of art forms. There were even competencies developed from oral histories shared between members by means of life lessons. In this way, there was a beautiful interplay between the attachment that occurred between members and the passing of stories with embedded knowledge, wisdom, and skills that led to competencies.

Life Arenas

Both the attachment and competencies gained throughout Witherspoon's project were directly connected to the areas of life the congregation cared about most. For this congregation, addressing connection during a time of social distancing was achieved via virtual platforms, outdoor worship, and theater such that isolation and despair did not prevail.

Their project also responded directly to the real-life arena of racism, homophobia, and other forms of social injustice. At a time in history when the reality of anti-Black racism and the value of LGBTQ+ lives are still debated, this congregation took a stand to support and take action around these causes and value all lives.

Congregational Practices

Congregational practices that were vehicles for transformation included worship, preaching, speaking, choir, vacation Bible school, artistic artifacts that adorned sacred spaces, and several other art forms. In fact, Pastor Harrison-Jones says that the project was engaged with all areas of the congregational practices of the church in some way. For example, he stated that the ability to trust one another, share, and feel connected shaped the liturgy, Bible studies, vacation Bible school, and every facet of congregational life.

Additionally, I celebrated with this congregation the cultural shifts described as outcomes of this project, outcomes that enabled people to desire to grow and to check one another and protect one another even amid differences. There was a sense of ownership and investment Harrison-Jones described that was prevalent throughout the membership. It warmed my heart to have heard that the Imani Wellness Project was voted on, with unanimous agreement that it be continued at Witherspoon Presbyterian Church.

Now then, how might you form a more creative congregation?

QUESTIONS FOR REFLECTION

1. What aspects of Witherspoon's congregational story connect with yours?

2. How might creativity provide a spark that lights a new path in your congregation?

NOTES

1. Shagun Singha, Melissa Warr, Punya Mishra, Danah Henriksen, and the Deep-Play Research Group, "Playing with Creativity across the Lifespan: A Conversation with Dr. Sandra Russ," *TechTrends* 64, no. 4 (May 2020): 550–54, https://doi.org/10.1007/s11528-020-00514-3.

2. Daniel H. Bowen and Brian Kisida, *Investigating Causal Effects of Arts Education Experiences: Experimental Evidence from Houston's Arts Access Initiative* (Houston: Rice University Kinder Institute for Urban Research, 2019), https://files.eric.ed.gov/fulltext/ED598203.pdf.

3. Singha et al., "Playing with Creativity," 550–54.

4. Saghir Ahmad, Abid Hussain Ch, Ayesha Batool, Khadija Sittar, and Misbah Malik, "Play and Cognitive Development: Formal Operational Perspective of Piaget's Theory," *Journal of Education and Practice* 7, no. 28 (2016): 72–79, https://files.eric.ed.gov/fulltext/EJ1118552.pdf.

5. Keith Sawyer, "The Cognitive Neuroscience of Creativity: A Critical Review," *Creativity Research Journal* 23, no. 2 (2011): 137–54, https://doi.org/10.1080/10400419.2011.571191.

6. Heather L. Stuckey and Jeremy Nobel, "The Connection between Art, Healing, and Public Health: A Review of Current Literature," *American Journal of Public Health* 100, no. 2 (2009): 254–63, https://doi.org/10.2105/ajph.2008.156497.

7. John Bowlby, *Attachment and Loss*, vol. 1, *Attachment* (New York: Basic Books, 1969).

8. Stéphane Guétin, Florence Portet, Marie-Christine Picot, C. Pommié, Mohsen Messaoudi, Leila Jemmi-Djabelkir, A. L. Olsen, M. M. Cano, Edith Lecourt, and Jacques Touchon, "Effect of Music Therapy on Anxiety and Depression in Patients with Alzheimer's Type Dementia: Randomised, Controlled Study," *Dementia and Geriatric Cognitive Disorders* 28, no. 1 (2009): 36–46, https://doi.org/10.1159/000229024.

9. Mihaly Csikszentmihalyi, "The Flow of Creativity," in *Creativity: Flow and the Psychology of Discovery and Invention*, 107–26 (New York: HarperCollins, 1996).

10. Ravenna Helson and Christopher J. Soto, "Up and Down in Middle Age: Monotonic and Nonmonotonic Changes in Roles, Status, and Personality,"

Journal of Personality and Social Psychology 89, no. 2 (2005): 194–204, https://doi.org/10.1037/0022-3514.89.2.194.

11. The Black Lives Matter street mural on Indiana Avenue in Indianapolis was created with contributions from eighteen artists. Each letter was created by a different artist as follows:
- #: Jarrod Dortch
- B: Nathaniel Rhodes
- L: Rebecca Robinson (PSNOB)
- A: Amiah Mims
- C: Billy Hoodoo
- K: Kevin Wes
- L: John G. Moore
- I: Gary Gee
- V: Deonna Craig
- E: Rae Parker
- S: Ess McKee
- M: Wavy Blayne
- A: Harriet Watson
- T: Shane Young (FITZ)
- T: Israel Solomon
- E: Shamira Wilson
- R: Ashley Nora
- Fist: Kenneth Hordge (Fingercreations)

12. "Indiana Avenue," Discover Indiana, https://publichistory.iupui.edu/items/show/242 (accessed September 1, 2023).

13. Teodros Kiros, ed., *Explorations in African Political Thought: Identity, Community, Ethics* (New York: Routledge, 2013).

14. Winterbourne Harrison-Jones, *Final Formative Power Grant Report*, Witherspoon Presbyterian Church (2021).

15. Harrison-Jones, *Final Report*.

16. Gil Bailie, *Violence Unveiled: Humanity at the Crossroads* (New York: Crossroad Publishing Company, 1995).

Chapter 8

Formative Power Imagined
A Case Study and Project Guide

This chapter is an imagined case study, a composite of many of the formative projects we've witnessed. We will call the congregation Hope Church, a faith community of one hundred located in the heart of Maplewood, a small neighborhood located within a larger city.

We have told stories of congregations and their application of the formative principles. Now we want to provide you with an example of what a formative process is like in a congregation. Our case study will be followed by a step-by-step guide to use with your congregation. We use the imagined congregation called Hope Church to provide context. Though Hope Church is imagined, the process is consistent with what congregations that took part in the Formative Power of Your Congregation designed for their experiences. While there is no single set of directions for designing a formative process, our goal is for Hope Church's story to provide you with ideas about how to create formative experiences for and with your congregation. Perhaps this story will empower you to design a Formative Power process that resonates with your congregation's unique rhythm and context.

A BEGINNING

Two deacons in Hope Church read and discussed the introduction of this book. They prepared the governing board to consider the formative experience. At the council meeting, one of the deacons described the principles of thinking of a congregation as a place of human development, paraphrasing the following from this book:

> The principle that underpins Formative Power is that God's purpose for our congregation is not merely numerical growth—it's the development of human beings. The formative process aspires to show our congregation how to ask, "What gifts do we have that can make a difference in individuals' lives, and how do we share them?" The Formative Power process is a learning experience that will help our congregation look away from self-preservation and look toward being a transformative presence in people's lives. (written by Kelly Minas, executive director of Center for Congregations' Center Evaluation and Funded Programs)

The council granted permission for the two deacons to create a formative team of between seven to ten members. The lead clergyperson stated that she supported this endeavor and would like to be on the team, though she did not want to facilitate the group.

At the team's first meeting, members were introduced to the meaning of life arenas.

The group was asked to identify an aspect of life that many in the congregation cared about, one aspect of life beyond the upkeep of the congregation. The formative team leaders described the concept of life arenas, various aspects of life that we occupy day to day. The task was to uncover life arenas that were of particular interest to church members. Examples of life arenas were offered (parenting, social justice, vocation, and more).

Hope Church opted to use an interview approach, listening to others share what areas of life most engaged them. High school students interviewed twenty church participants, prompting them to share stories about meaningful life experiences related to their personal values. The analysis revealed a recurring theme: the majority of interviewees told stories about elders or mentors who'd had a positive lifelong influence on the interviewees. Also, more than half of the interviewees were public school teachers, educators who felt that teaching to the whole person, not only teaching the subject matter, was essential to education. This insight informed the formative team's decision to focus their formative project on what it means to mentor others, what it means to be an "elder."

The next step was for the team to combine the life arena of mentoring with congregational practices that support the positive dynamics of mentoring. The team leaders shared a handout with a list of congregational practices that are common to congregations. This sheet illustrated what was meant by congregational practices: congregational practices refer to activities commonly observed in churches, including preaching, teaching, caring for souls, affiliation, and more. Many churches demonstrate the same practices, but the practices have unique expression from congregation to congregation.

Hope Church's team combined the life arena of mentoring with a current high school youth group activity, a specific congregation practice. Each high school student in the youth group was matched with an adult to encourage intergenerational relationships and informal opportunities for faith exploration. This matching and mentoring was in its third year, and participants enjoyed spending time with one another. This congregational practice was the most frequently mentioned activity when considering the life arena of mentoring. In the formative process, it is common for a life arena to be a readily apparent match with one or more congregational practices. Such was the case with Hope Church. The youth group mentoring activities matched well with congregants' interests in mentoring.

The team then added another activity. One project leader pointed out that the newest adult education class was called News of the Week. The class, with anywhere from eight to twelve in attendance, chose a topic in the news the week prior and discussed the topic in light of the members' understanding of the Gospel. Sometimes the conversations revealed agreement (the school board should not ban books written by the author John Green, for example *The Fault in Our Stars*[1]).

On one occasion, the News of the Week conversation was intense and chipped away at civility, leaving some participants hurt or at least unhappy. This particular week the group talked about an issue that was uncharacteristically controversial for the group (usually the class chose the news of the week from feature columns about people or from reviews of movies). The controversial topic was about a state court ruling on abortion. The discussion started respectfully ("I can see your point of view") and then regressed into judgment ("How can you call yourself a Christian?"). Despite this kind of occasional intensity, the formative team agreed that the class was essential to the congregation's commitment to honoring diverse opinions.

The team opted to preserve the relational aspect of mentoring, creating a distinct space alongside it for another life arena: education, or lifelong learning as they interchangeably called it. One member aptly captured the team's spirit, saying, "I can't imagine ever stopping the journey of learning." Compared to the relational focus of mentoring, education (among team members) emphasized the cognitive aspects of development. Furthermore, the team's decision to include the News of the Week adult Sunday school class along with the youth group mentoring program exemplifies how formative teams often uncover new areas for exploration as they progress.

Now the Formative Power team had two aspects of the process identified: life arenas in the form of mentoring and education/lifelong learning and congregational practices in the form of mentoring and current event exploration. At this point, Hope Church's team provided a progress report to the oversight council. Timely reports to other groups in the congregation or to the congregation overall are good practice in the formative process.

So, the third stage of Hope Church's formative process focused on trail markers—how these markers connect with life arenas (areas where faith intersects with daily life) and congregational practices (activities within the church). The goal was to design formative experiences that integrated these three elements. The team learned that trail markers represented character traits, like attachment and competence, that represent Hope Church members growing closer to their full potential as humans. This aligns with the church's mission—to support well-lived lives, not just participation in committees. The facilitators provided the group with a list of trail markers and their definitions.

The team chose attachment as a trail marker because of the importance of relationships to learning. The team also selected self-differentiation because learning in the context of difficult discussions about divisive events requires the ability to state what one believes and yet leaves room for others to disagree. Finally, the group chose the trail marker of integration because making sense of divisive events requires absorbing the good and the bad from such events. Plus, team members noted that reconciling good and bad, virtues and vices, involves maturity. It takes wisdom to face that which is disappointing in oneself.

At this point, the Hope Church team started planning their program by exploring important theological ideas. The pastor helped by explaining concepts from womanist and existential theology, with examples to make them clear.

Regarding womanist theology, the pastor highlighted the transformative power of female relationships, particularly among women of color who navigate systemic obstacles and encounter indifference (or worse) when seeking support for or recognition of their unique bond. The immediacy and priority of mutual respect and solidarity among women often defies societal norms regarding "getting ahead" and hiding from difficult experiences. Stories told in the spirit of womanist theology highlight friendship and kinship, fostering resilience and courage. The pastor asked, "What relationships in church or in life beyond church do you enjoy that defy societal norms?"

Additionally, the pastor defined existential theology for the group. She asked individuals in the group to think about what is most important to them. What joy does it bring? In what ways does it feel overwhelming? The pastor explained that existential theology is a way to think about how you experience your faith (or not) via what matters most to you. When you are considering that which matters most to you and your faith, you are, in a sense, an existential theologian. Recall important experiences. How are such important experiences essential to your development as a person of faith? Do you feel anxious? Do you feel disconnected? Or do you feel that in certain situations, this is "the real you"?

With all this in mind, the Hope Church team crafted a sentence summarizing the group's work: "We have identified mentoring and education as our life arenas, informed by our congregational practices of our high school mentoring project and our News of the Week class to provide developmental growth regarding attachment, self-differentiation, and integration."

The Hope Church team brainstormed ideas for activities aligned with their chosen triad of life arenas, congregational practices, and trail markers. They prioritized their choices based on consensus, noting which ideas sparked the most interest (and energy). They selected the most promising activity ideas and refined them into specific formative activities.

With a clear direction in place, Hope Church was ready to put their Formative Program into action. Their implementation process included creating a detailed schedule, assigning tasks to specific people, figuring out the budget, and defining what success would look like. Let's now turn to the details of implementing their Formative Program.

THE CONGREGATION IMPLEMENTS THEIR FORMATIVE PROGRAM

So, based on what life arenas, congregational practices, and trail markers most resonated with Hope Church leaders, it was time to implement a program of activities that would foster the human development of congregants. Their Formative Program is described below.

Intergenerational Meetups Spark Connections and Conversations

The formative team designed an activity they called meetups. This activity encouraged members to connect with someone from a different generation, preferably someone not in the congregation. This could be as simple as lunch or coffee. The council provided ten dollars per participating church member as a gesture of support, covering some of the cost of a meal or cups of coffee.

News of the Day Events Spark Reflection and Dialogue

Three News of the Day events were planned:

- *School board visit:* participants would attend a school board meeting as observers, fostering community engagement.
- *Local history dinner:* a speaker from the historical society would discuss a challenging period in the area's history, such as school desegregation.
- *Meaningful yet difficult field trip:* a trip to a site representing a contested issue of the past (a location of gun violence) to spark dialogue about difficult topics, including *how* to talk about difficult

topics. This event proved challenging, with only five participants due to the sensitive nature of the topic.

Fellowship Meals Unpack Experiences and Growth

Focusing on all of the activities, the formative team facilitated discussions at three fellowship events to reflect on their formative activities. These events included:

- a shared meal
- participant stories about their experiences
- a relevant Scripture study
- discussion about how the chosen trail markers were experienced by participants

These key questions were offered and discussed at each event:

1. What were the positive experiences? What were the challenges?
2. How did this program make a difference in your congregation? What was the difference?
3. How were you formed personally? What other stories of personal formation were there?

Diverse Reactions and Growth Opportunities

The neighborly intergenerational invitations elicited mixed responses. Meeting neighbors from different generations felt awkward for some. It meant talking to people they only knew from a wave at the mailbox, not their usual social circle. Yet those who took the initiative found conversations warming up and friendships forming.

Subsequent connections ranged from sharing brownies and sending and receiving thank-you notes, to additional visits and surprise gifts. One participant said, "I may not be best friends with this person, but I feel close and even warm when I hear their name." Another noted, "I met with an older adult, and we had plenty to talk about and still have more" (remember the concept of unlimited conversation).

The school board visit, however, generated cynicism and tension among participants. The pastor and a formative team member went to dinner with two congregation members who disagreed regarding consideration of textbooks, ultimately leading to an agreement to disagree, a gesture toward self-differentiation.

The trip to the site of gun violence also sparked mixed reactions. Some felt conflicted about reconciling their safe lives with the violent witness they couldn't ignore. One person remarked, "I try not to think of these things," while another countered, "I must think of these things. I figure where we live has both good and evil, like the Garden of Eden." This participant also felt that the News of the Week topics were too soft and suggested tackling more challenging issues, like they had when they discussed the court ruling on abortion.

Refocusing and Moving Forward

The church council voted to continue the formative process but to shift its focus. Recognizing the challenges of complex markers like integration and self-differentiation, they decided to continue the intergenerational meetups, but this time within the congregation, encouraging pairs to form by choice. The council also incorporated testimonies about these connections during worship services.

Additionally, and somewhat unexpectedly, the News of the Week class, on their own, decided to purposely choose, once a month, a controversial, even polarizing topic to study and discuss. As one member asked, "If we can't talk about tough things at church, where can we?"

WHAT ABOUT YOUR CONGREGATION?

We have peeled back the layers of congregational life to reveal its transformative potential, illuminated a path toward becoming communities of faith that nurture healthy and thriving human beings, and imagined Hope Church doing so using the formative power framework. We now extend an open invitation to you, our readers, to join us on this ongoing journey of formation as well. We hope that you feel well equipped with the insights and knowledge to be active, intentional, and creative stewards of the formative power within your congregations. To further aid you toward this end, what follows is a summative guide from start to finish for conducting your own Formative Power project.

If you have been mulling over the reflection questions at the end of each chapter, then you have already started dreaming about what formative powers your congregation holds! Your next steps are below. Remember, the guiding claim and question for this project is that God's purpose for your congregation is development of human beings, and how can your congregation be a transformative presence in people's lives?

THE FORMATIVE POWER OF YOUR CONGREGATION: A GUIDE

Step 1: Create a Formative Power team.

- This could be a team of seven to ten people.
- The team could include pastor(s), lay leaders, or any otherwise engaged members.
- This process could be commenced as a singular congregation or with other congregations in collaboration.

Step 2: Host your first gathering and begin with a brief description of Formative Power such as the one here:

The principle that underpins Formative Power is that God's purpose for our congregation is not growth—it's the development of human beings. The formative process aspires to show our congregation how to ask, "What gifts do we have that can make a difference in individuals' lives, and how do we share them?" The Formative Power process is a learning experience that will help our congregation look away from self-preservation and look toward being a transformative presence in people's lives.

Step 3: Introduce life arenas as the first dimension of this project as illustrated in figure 8.1. Ask the group to identify an aspect of life that many in the congregation care about beyond the upkeep of the congregation. Include the list of examples below.

Life Arena Examples

- *Family:* An essential unit of society, typically consisting of parents and their children. Family can include relatives, adopted family members, and anyone considered close and supportive.
- *Vocation:* A calling or occupation, possibly one's purpose in life.
- *Finances:* The management of money and other assets.
- *Wellness:* A state of vigor encompassing physical, mental, emotional, spiritual, and social health.
- *The arts:* Activities involving creative undertakings, such as visual arts, music, literature, dance, theater, and film.
- *Education:* The process of gaining knowledge and skills through formal or informal instruction or learning experiences.
- *Social justice:* The equitable distribution of everyone's resources and rights, advocating freedom from discrimination, oppression, and inequality.

Figure 8.1 Life Arena

- *Being a neighbor:* Participating in and contributing to the well-being of a local community.
- *Care for the ill:* Providing physical, emotional, and social support to those who are sick or injured.
- *Charity:* The voluntary giving of time, money, or resources to help those in need.
- *Creation care:* Protecting and restoring the earth, recognizing its intrinsic and extrinsic values for human flourishing.
- *Mental health:* An individual's emotional, psychological, spiritual, and social well-being.
- *Parenting:* Raising a child and providing for their physical, emotional, and social needs, resulting in secure attachment.
- *Specific hobbies:* Activities pursued for enjoyment and personal fulfillment.
- *Teaching:* Sharing knowledge, skills, and understanding with others.

Step 4: Facilitate the following discussion with your team.

- What is a pain point in your life and/or the lives of those within the congregation?
- What is a real challenge in life for many right now?
- Share other important matters of your lives as examples of life arenas.

Step 5: Query the entire congregation using the following possible methods

Congregational Query

1. Church Survey
   - Develop a survey with the life arenas identified above (e.g., vocation, social justice, parenting).
   - Ask members to rank the life arenas in order of personal importance.
   - Ask your congregation's formative team to analyze the results and determine the top two to four life arenas for your project focus.

1. In-Depth Interviews
   - Select a dedicated group (this could include empowering a group of teens) to interview twenty congregants.
   - The interviews should invite congregants to tell a story about a time when a life experience significantly impacted their way of thinking or acting related to something truly important to them.
   - Notes should be taken, and the stories should be brought back to the planning team to analyze and to identify recurring themes and key life areas impacted by church practices.

Note about the benefits:

- Queries of this kind underscore the goal for this project to support the entire congregation rather than the concerns of a few.
- Hope Church knew that both methods provide valuable insights into the needs and aspirations of their congregation.
- Surveys offer a quantitative perspective, while interviews delve deeper into individual experiences and motivations.
- Using both methods could lead to a more comprehensive understanding and targeted project focus.

Step 6: Connect a life arena with congregational practices as reflected in figure 8.2. A partial list of examples is provided.

Partial List of Congregational Practices

- *Preaching:* Proclamation of faith based on an interpretation of Scripture, typically the sermon during worship.
- *Worship:* The act of a faith community gathering to praise God through hymns, Scripture readings, prayer, offerings, and more.
- *Music:* Song or sound rooted in the larger faith story of human beings, sometimes by the entire congregation, a soloist, or choir members.
- *Bible study:* Learning, typically with others, the content of Scripture and the meaning that content has for life.
- *Travel:* Any number of journeys congregants go on, usually a subset of the entire assembly traveling to a mission site to support others, or going on a spiritual retreat or to a site for faith education.

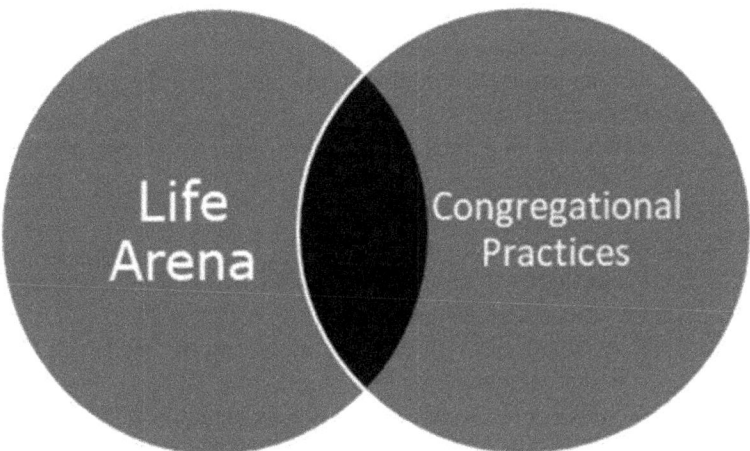

Figure 8.2 Life Arena and Congregational Practices

- *Fellowship meals:* Any number of activities hosted by a congregation where people eat together, sometimes on a regular basis, like every Wednesday evening, and sometimes for special occasions like church anniversaries, honoring clergy, and so forth.
- *Sacraments and rites of passage:* Congregations, depending on their living tradition, offer sacred acts like baptism or communion representing God's saving grace or sustaining love.
- *Care ministries:* A variety of interpersonal activities where either mutual support is offered or a clergyperson, deacon, or other person offers care for another's spiritual and personal well-being, sometimes called the care of souls, taking place at the church site or home, or in a hospital or other location.

Step 7: Identify specific congregational practices that inform your life arena by following the suggested process below.

Connecting Life Arenas and Congregational Practice

1. Identifying Congregational Practices
   1.1. Brainstorming
      - Examine the list of practices.

- Identify existing practices not in the list (special services, movie nights, mentoring, etc.).
- Encourage other additions and ideas from the group.
1.2. Refine the list
- Discuss and then finalize key congregational practices to consider.
2. Juxtaposing with Life Arenas
   2.1. Divide into small groups
   - Create two to three teams with three to four members each.
   2.2. Provide materials to each team
   - A large yellow sheet to be posted on the wall with "life arena" written at the top.
   - Sticky notes on which to write congregational practices.
   2.3. Juxtaposition activity
   - The small teams arrange congregational practice sticky notes on the yellow sheet.
   - Discuss connections and conflicts between the life arena and practices.
   - Ask, which practices connect? Which clash?
   2.4. Storytelling
   - Each team chooses two members.
   - One tells a story of a harmonious juxtaposition (match).
   - The other tells a story of a discordant juxtaposition (not a match).
   - Encourage vivid storytelling.
   - Choose the most expressive juxtapositions between mentoring and congregational practice(s).
3. Sharing and Consensus
   3.1. The whole group reconvenes
   - Bring everyone back together.
   3.2. Each team presents
   - Teams present their chosen juxtaposition and linked story.
   3.3. Affirmation
   - Leaders affirm all stories and contributions.
   3.4. Reaching consensus:
   - Discuss presented juxtapositions as a whole group.

- Encourage active listening, open-ended questions, and honest discussion.
- Aim for consensus on the most inspiring or moving combination.

* Remember, improvisation and adjustments are welcome throughout the process. That is, the entire group might choose congregational practices that had not been previously named, or life arenas other than mentoring may be named as important.

Step 8: Gather the team to explore trail markers that could be addressed by congregational practices and life arena focus as shown in figure 8.3. Share the list and definitions below.

Trail Markers

- *Attachment:* The ability to have healthy relationships in which you are your best and truest self. Through positive relationships you are able to get essential needs like safety, truth telling, forgiveness, trust, and more met. Your growth is enhanced through life in community.
- *Emotional regulation:* The capacity to experience, name, express, and act in the midst of positive and painful emotions in a way over which you have agency. You have emotions; the emotions don't have you. Likewise, you can be in tune with the emotions of others and hold those emotions without being swept away.
- *Self-differentiation:* The ability to experience oneself as separate from others or to "differentiate" oneself, with personal values, thoughts, feelings, and choices, while at the same time remaining in relationship with those who are in any number of ways distinct from you.
- *Initiative:* The ability to be resourceful in relationship to the challenges and opportunities faced in life. One is not passive but uses creativity and talents to accomplish goals and help others to be proactive as well.
- *Transcendence:* The realization that life is larger than oneself, that one is part of a reality greater than the self. The experience

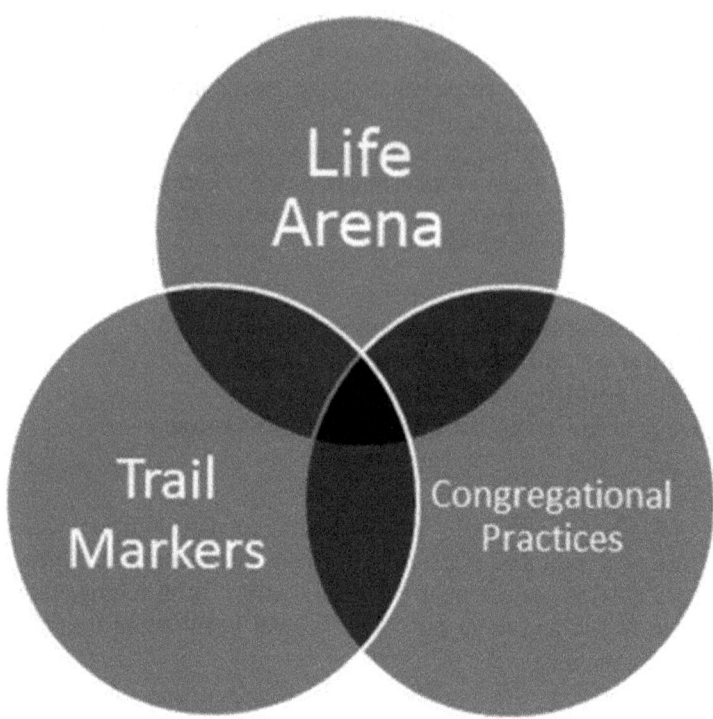

Figure 8.3 Arena Markers Practices Venn Diagram

of finding and contributing to meaning, purpose, and an ultimate concern beyond oneself.
- *Competence:* Competence has to do with identifying and developing one's skills and gifts. Such ability applies to numerous life arenas including school, household, vocation, civic life, and family. Competence involves learning how to do certain activities and how to think strategically about situations and systems.
- *Authority:* This is the experience of seeing others as equal and mutual, especially authority figures. It involves being able to "own" one's power and acknowledge the authority of others in ways that don't diminish oneself.
- *Integration:* The experience of reconciling negative aspects of life, such as losses, imperfection, sin, and pain, along with the positive, such as love, success, and accomplishment.

Step 9: Use the suggested process below for putting together life arenas, congregational practices, and trail markers.

1. Review the Trail Markers
   Read and discuss: Review the trail markers together and identify which markers led to the most questions and discussion.
   Story sharing: If one marker sparks significant questions, the team facilitator can invite a story about who helped such growth develop. For instance, was it a family member, a friend, or perhaps a stranger who was the incubator for growth? Who has helped you become the best you?
2. Self-Reflection
   Personal experiences: Participants share their experiences of a trail marker, a marker of their inner life and nearly being satisfied with their functioning in various situations.
3. Juxtaposition Revisited
   Visualizing connections: Prepare sticky notes representing your two life arenas and the trail markers described above.
   Silent reflection: Two minutes allotted for individual reflection on which trail markers might be fostered by the chosen congregational practices to support the identified life arenas. What trail markers might be most important to navigating the two life arenas supported by the identified congregational practices?
   Group discussion: The group collaboratively decides which two trail markers best align with the combined life arena and congregational practices.
4. Theological Connection
   Scriptural reference: Try to identify a Bible verse or narrative that embodies this "trinity" of life arena, practices, and trail markers.
   Theological theme: Explore relevant theological themes with your group.
5. Action Steps
   Summarize findings: Craft a sentence summarizing the group's work. For example, "We have identified mentoring and responding to current events as our life arenas, informed by our congregational practices of our high school mentoring project and our News of the Week class to provide growth regarding attachment, self-differentiation, and integration.

Brainstorm activities: Brainstorm ideas for activities aligned with the chosen "triad" of life arenas, congregational practices, and trail markers. Prioritize choices based on consensus, noting which ideas sparked the most interest (and energy). Select the most promising activity ideas and refine them into specific formative activities.

Implementation: Create a thorough implementation plan for formative activities by establishing a timeline, assigning responsibilities, determining a budget, and defining success.

Step 9 concludes the formal process but is most certainly not the end of the journey. We hope the steps we have charted guide and support you along the way. With each step, we pray there will be discoveries and formative experiences awaiting each congregation willing to trust the process.

NOTE

1. John Green, *The Fault in Our Stars* (New York: Penguin, 2012).

Chapter 9

Transforming Individuals, Transforming Communities

In this chapter, we aim to synthesize the insights and transformative experiences explored throughout this book. We have embarked on a quest to understand how congregations harness the power to form healthy and thriving human beings. Now, as we reflect on our exploration, we will highlight key takeaways and articulate hopes for the future of faith communities and their formative power.

Throughout this book, we have sought to lay the groundwork for a comprehensive curriculum that supports an ongoing praxis of transformative congregational life. In doing so, we have been guided by the conviction that God's purpose for congregations goes beyond building maintenance and numerical church growth, but for us to grow as human beings and for congregations to be places that help us do so in powerful, Spirit-inspired ways. We have dared to envision congregations as communities of creative resistance, where the transformative power of faith challenges the status quo in society and beckons us to be persons who continue to reach and work toward a more just and compassionate world.[1]

To achieve this, we began by delving into the rich tapestry of theological reflection on congregational life in chapter 1, examining it through the lenses of theology, pastoral theology, and ecclesiology. Contextual ecclesiology served as the most helpful framework to honor the lived experiences of beliefs, identity, congregational activity, and existential theology, and womanist theology and provided a lens with which to engage context in this way.

We then introduced the concept of life arenas as areas of life that congregants care about most. Life arenas are focal points for growth and support within congregations. Then we explored the transformative impact and potential of congregational practices that make up the life of the church such as prayer, testimony, song, and sacraments.

Lastly, we borrowed insights from human development and developmental psychology to outline eight trail markers of development, providing a language to describe growth and indicators that help tell us how we know when we grow.

As we look back at our journey, we've witnessed congregations engaging in profound acts of formation. In chapter 5, we shared the story of congregations grappling with racial reconciliation, demonstrating how emotional regulation, integration, authority, and competence served as guiding trail markers in their transformative journey.

In chapter 6, we explored how a congregation's initiative in Learn-Go-Do education groups led to strengthened relationships and a deeper connection with their community, guided by the markers of attachment, initiative, competence, and self-regulation.

Finally, in chapter 7, we delved into the world of arts with one congregation where intergenerational connection, competence, and attachment played crucial roles in nurturing zeal for life and making a stance on matters of justice for all.

While we could not share every Formative Power congregational story within this text, we, along with an incredible team, were intentional along the way to bear witness to and reflect on the experiences of each congregation and cohort. After listening and reflecting, here are a few themes we would like to share.

KEY THEMES

Among the key themes was the fact that formative projects often reflected a journey of faith that aligned with a congregation's own history.[2] In each instance, the Formative Power projects are designed to help members continue to seek the face of God in unlikely places—Northside New Era discovering the Ku Klux Klan paraphernalia in their newly acquired church building and later traveling to Cincinnati to the National Underground Railroad Freedom Center, and Good Samaritan leveraging its progressive and inclusive/equality values and "seeking Christ in all persons, loving your neighbor" (based on the Baptismal Covenant) through diverse study groups.

Another key theme that emerged from reflecting on these projects was the importance of disruptive, or liminal, experiences. While there was a lot of diversity among the projects conducted, what most projects had in common was that they surpassed a critical threshold of disrupting the normative practices and activities of the congregations. In some cases, this included traveling; in others, difficult, never-before-had conversations; and in other cases, a yearlong season of experimenting with new ways of being and doing. In this way, the projects were ripe for facilitating transformation due to the ways they challenged long-held beliefs and created openings for experiential learning. As one congregation stated, "This project really helped me to learn what I needed to throw out and pick up in terms of how to help connect those dots between that Baptismal Covenant and practical living of our theology on the ground."

Several participants shared what was described as a "loss of control" as a positive effect of their formative work. For example, liminal experiences were described in terms of being not in control or being outside a comfort zone. One participant said it was useful to "get people in spaces that allow them to not be in charge." Another took this as a lesson about the kind of life a project like Formative Power must take in a congregation: "It proved that when relationships are really forming and connection is really forming, you can't always control that in a linear way."

We learned that an important aspect of how liminal experiences make way for growth was the presence of just enough emotional safety while experiencing that which was new and troubling. Emotional safety was often represented by friendships, congregational practices, and learning difficult truths in the sanctuary of a museum. Liminal experiences plus a holding environment equal human development. A holding environment may be a place, a feeling, or a state of mind. When we are in one, we feel safe and supported, like we can let down our guard and be ourselves. This lets us connect with others on a deeper level and grow.[3]

It was also noted that two external disruptions played into all Formative Power projects. First, the George Floyd murder in May 2020 had a profound impact on all congregations and in all cases provided the impetus to focus on racial justice, dismantling white supremacy, and working toward reconciliation. Secondly, the COVID-19 pandemic was a challenging disruption to all congregations in terms of project implementation. Yet congregations spoke all the more of needing to exercise many of the trail markers of human development as they worked to adapt.

Many of the cohort leaders interviewed even identified hopeful approaches and beneficial impacts despite the pandemic. Multiple participants remarked that, while certainly a challenging circumstance, the pandemic allowed them to do activities, pursue themes, or form relationships that they might not have otherwise considered.[4] As one interviewee said, "Not being in person allowed talents to sprout" in unique ways. One congregation had to cancel a trip but then rescheduled and expanded the trip opportunity to the whole diocese, not just their church, and thus more participants produced greater results. Certainly, COVID-19 created suffering beyond what could have been predicted in 2019. However, congregational resilience produced unexpected impacts. The connection between resilience and human development is real and observable.

Lastly, many participants shared with us that the Formative learning cohort was essential to their positive experiences. Having a community of congregational leaders doing the same kinds of activities and confronting the same challenges was highly appreciated by these participants. "Accountability" and "collegiality" were terms used to describe the benefits of learning alongside others.

Even this far along in the journey of this book, it is good and right to remember our premise. Participation in a congregation can and should be more than a list of demands, say, worship attendance, pledging, or volunteering to be an usher. These activities certainly have their place, but the conditions of religious commitments call for more. Such conditions call for experiences that point to an expansive horizon beyond one's own vision. In this way, participation in congregational life can be reframed from being about the labor of volunteers who support an institution to belonging to a community that supports human development consistent with espoused beliefs.

Belonging is a basic human need. It begins from the first day of life when humans begin to attach (or not attach) with parents. A reconsideration of religious community can be more than an exploration to reassess the relevance of membership. Congregations rethinking membership can be an opportunity to provide secure attachment with the Divine and with a people. Such secure attachment makes it more possible, our hypothesis goes, for congregants to live into the full stature of the community's religious claims and commitments (Ephesians 4:13).

What if congregations dared to rethink their purpose? What if your congregation adopted habits bold enough to teach you that the heart and the hurt of your experiences create the conditions for the development you seek to fully experience the challenges and highlights of life? So, resilience isn't just a virtue; it's a sign of growth, and growth signifies hope (Romans 5:4). Imagine your church where membership isn't a chore but an invitation to become more fully human, an ongoing and essential call for us all; your congregation is a community that looks as far as the stars for the ground of being. This is a formative opportunity for us all. What would it mean for a congregation to rethink its reason for living? It might mean taking on habits and routines grand enough to experience that suffering produces endurance, trusting that endurance produces character, and character produces hope (Romans 5:4).

Carrying such hope opens a person to experiences of transcendence, reminders that one is not the center of the universe, that indeed one is part of a much larger reality that extends from the past, to the present, to a beyond that ignites imagination.

YOU ARE INVITED

We acknowledge that the journey is far from over. The stories we've shared, the concepts we've introduced, and the wisdom we've gained are not static entities but dynamic forces for change. The transformative power of congregations is an ongoing, ever-evolving process. So, where do we go from here?

Our hope is to inspire communities of faith to become active, intentional, and creative stewards of their formative power. We believe that by equipping those who participate in congregational life with the tools, resources, and stories we've provided in this book, we can catalyze a ripple effect of transformation. When nurtured, congregations, like the individuals in them, have the capacity to evolve, adapt, and thrive.

A VISION FOR THE FUTURE

In the future, we envision faith communities embracing their role as agents of growth and change in an increasingly high-pressure, complex world. We hope to see congregations continually reflect on and identify the formative power they hold, not just within their walls but in the broader communities they touch. We aspire to witness congregations embracing the challenges of our times, from issues of racial justice to environmental stewardship, with a commitment to growth, wellness, and support of human beings and creation.

Throughout this journey, we have often been reminded of the words of Howard Thurman, theologian and civil rights leader, who said, "Don't ask what the world needs. Ask what makes you come alive, and go do it. Because what the world needs is people who have come alive."[5] Congregations, as centers of spiritual vitality, have the potential to make people come alive in profound ways. In the future, we envision faith communities not only as places of worship but as catalysts for growth and transformation. Join us on an ongoing journey of formation. Together, we can continue to transform lives and, in turn, transform communities.

QUESTIONS FOR REFLECTION

1. Have you been on a trip or retreat as part of a congregation? If so, what feelings and stories do you recall?
2. What has been one of the most disorienting experiences you've had as part of a congregation, a time when you felt, say, out of your element?

NOTES

1. Walter Brueggemann, *The Prophetic Imagination* (Philadelphia: Fortress Press, 1978).
2. Susan M. Weber, director, Evaluation and Communication Project, Center for Congregations, citing written reflections, 2021.

3. Donald W. Winnicott, *The Maturational Processes and the Facilitating Environment: Studies in the Theory of Emotional Development* (New York: Routledge, 2018).

4. Kelly Minas, director for center evaluation, Center for Congregations, citing excerpts from written program evaluation reflections, 2021.

5. Howard Thurman, quoted in Gil Bailie, *Violence Unveiled: Humanity at the Crossroads* (New York: Crossroad Publishing Company, 1995), xv. Gil Bailie tells this story in the first paragraph of the "In Gratitude" section of his book: "Once, when I was seeking the advice of Howard Thurman and talking to him at some length about what needed to be done in the world, he interrupted me and said, 'Don't ask yourself what the world needs. Ask yourself what makes you come alive, and go do that, because what the world needs is people who have come alive.'" This is the only known print location of this quote.

Bibliography

Adams, Christopher J., Holly Hough, Rae Jean Proeschold-Bell, Jia Yao, and Melanie Kolkin. "Clergy Burnout: A Comparison Study with Other Helping Professions." *Pastoral Psychology* 66 (July 2016): 147–75. https://doi.org/10.1007/s11089-016-0722-4.

Ahmad, Saghir, Abid Hussain Ch, Ayesha Batool, Khadija Sittar, and Misbah Malik. "Play and Cognitive Development: Formal Operational Perspective of Piaget's Theory." *Journal of Education and Practice* 7, no. 28 (2016): 72–79. https://files.eric.ed.gov/fulltext/EJ1118552.pdf.

Bailie, Gil. *Violence Unveiled: Humanity at the Crossroads*. New York: Crossroad Publishing Company, 1995.

Barber, William. *We Are Called to Be a Movement*. New York: Workman Publishing, 2020.

Barnes, Sandra L., Lauren Brinkley-Rubinstein, Bernadette Doykos, Nina C. Martin, and Alison McGuire. *Academics in Action! A Model for Community-Engaged Research, Teaching, and Service*. New York: Fordham University Press, 2016.

Battle, Michael. *Reconciliation: The Ubuntu Theology of Desmond Tutu*. Rev. ed. Cleveland: Pilgrim Press, 2009.

Berry, Wendell. *What Are People For?* San Francisco: North Point Press, 1990.

———. *The Wild Birds*. San Francisco: North Point Press, 1986.

Bolz-Weber, Nadia. *Accidental Saints: Finding God in All the Wrong People*. New York: Convergent Books, 2015.

———. *Pastrix: The Cranky, Beautiful Faith of a Sinner & Saint*. New York: Hachette, 2013.

Bonhoeffer, Dietrich. *Letters and Papers from Prison*. Dietrich Bonhoeffer Works 8. Minneapolis: Fortress Press, 2010.

———. *Life Together: The Classic Exploration of Christian Community*. New York: HarperCollins, 1954.

Boucher Pye, Amy. *7 Ways to Pray: Time-Tested Practices for Encountering God.* Colorado Springs: NavPress, 2021.

Bowen, Daniel H., and Brian Kisida. *Investigating Causal Effects of Arts Education Experiences: Experimental Evidence from Houston's Arts Access Initiative.* Houston: Rice University Kinder Institute for Urban Research, 2019. https://files.eric.ed.gov/fulltext/ED598203.pdf.

Bowlby, John. *Attachment and Loss.* New York: Basic Books, 1969.

Brooks, Arthur C. *From Strength to Strength: Finding Success, Happiness and Deep Purpose in the Second Half of Life.* New York: Portfolio/Penguin, 2022.

Brooks, David. *The Second Mountain: The Quest for a Moral Life.* New York: Random House, 2020.

Brueggemann, Walter. *The Prophetic Imagination.* Philadelphia: Fortress Press, 1978.

Buber, Martin. *I and Thou.* Edinburgh: T&T Clark, 1923.

Butler, Lee H., Jr. *Liberating Our Dignity, Saving Our Souls: A New Theory of African American Identity Formation.* St. Louis: Chalice Press, 2006.

Buttrick, David. *Preaching Jesus Christ: An Exercise in Homiletic Theology.* Eugene: Wipf and Stock, 2002.

———. *Speaking Conflict: Stories of a Controversial Jesus.* Louisville: Westminster John Knox Press, 2007.

Carroll College. "Vatican II." Accessed September 2, 2023. https://www.carroll.edu/about/history/catholic-history-heritage/vatican-ii.

Center for Congregations. "Learn Go Do: A Transformative Journey of Community Engagement." Accessed September 23, 2023. https://centerforcongregations.org/stories/learn-go-do-a-transformative-journey-of-community-engagement-at-main-street-umc.

Chaves, Mark. *Congregations in America.* Cambridge, MA: Harvard University Press, 2004.

Cooper-White, Pamela. "Human Development in Relational and Cultural Perspective." In *Human Development and Faith: Life-Cycle Stages of Body, Mind and Soul*, 80–102. St. Louis: Chalice Press, 2004.

Crossan, John Dominic. *The Historical Jesus: The Life of a Mediterranean Jewish Peasant.* New York: HarperCollins, 1991.

———. *The Power of Parable: How Fiction by Jesus Became Fiction about Jesus.* New York: HarperCollins, 2012.

Csikszentmihalyi, Mihaly. "The Flow of Creativity." In *Creativity: Flow and the Psychology of Discovery and Invention.* New York: HarperCollins, 1996.

Cunningham, David. *Christian Ethics: The End of the Law.* New York: Routledge, 2008.

Denworth, Lydia. *Friendship: The Evolution, Biology, and Extraordinary Power of Life's Fundamental Bond.* New York: Norton, 2020.

Doblmeier, Martin, dir. *Bonhoeffer.* Journey Films, 2003. 1 hr., 33 min. https://www.journeyfilms.com/store/p/bonhoeffer.

Dulles, Avery. *Models of the Church.* New York: Crown, 2002.

Dutta, Nayantara. "Why We Remember Music and Forget Everything Else." *Time*, April 14, 2022. Accessed September 2, 2023. https://time.com/6167197/psychology-behind-remembering-music.

DuVernay, Ava, dir. *Selma.* Paramount Pictures, 2014. DVD.

Dykstra, Craig. *Growing in the Life of Faith: Education and Christian Practices.* Louisville: Westminster John Knox Press, 1999.

———. *Growing in the Life of Faith: Education and Christian Practices.* 2nd ed. Louisville: Westminster John Knox Press, 2005.

Dykstra, Robert C. *Images of Pastoral Care: Classic Readings.* St. Louis: Chalice Press, 2005.

Evans, Nancy J., Deanna S. Forney, Florence M. Guido, Lori D. Patton, and Kristen A. Renn. *Student Development in College: Theory, Research, and Practice.* 2nd ed. San Francisco: Jossey-Bass, 2010.

Evans, Rachel Held. *Searching for Sunday: Loving, Leaving, and Finding the Church.* Nashville: Nelson Books, 2015.

Feliu-Soler, Albert, Juan C. Pascual, Xavier Borràs, Maria J. Portella, Ana Martín-Blanco, Antonio Armario, Enric Alvarez, Victor Pérez, and Joaquim Soler. "Effects of Dialectical Behaviour Therapy–Mindfulness Training on Emotional Reactivity in Borderline Personality Disorder: Preliminary Results." *Clinical Psychology & Psychotherapy* 21, no. 4 (March 2013): 363–70. https://doi.org/10.1002/cpp.1837.

Finlayson, Gordon. *Habermas: A Very Short Introduction.* New York: Oxford University Press, 2005.

Forgeard, Marie J. C. "Perceiving Benefits after Adversity: The Relationship between Self-Reported Posttraumatic Growth and Creativity." *Psychology of Aesthetics, Creativity, and the Arts* 7, no. 3 (2013): 245–64. https://dx.doi.org/10.1037/a0031223.

Foster, Jodie, dir. *Little Man Tate.* Orion Pictures, 1991. DVD.

Fowler, James W. *Stages of Faith: The Psychology of Human Development and the Quest for Meaning.* San Francisco: HarperOne, 1995.

Franco, Marisa G. *Platonic: How the Science of Attachment Can Help You Make—and Keep—Friends.* New York: Putnam, 2022.

Friedman, Edwin H. *Generation to Generation: Family Process in Church and Synagogue.* New York: Guilford, 1985.

———. "Paradox in Therapy, Paradox in Life." Center for Family Process, 1999. Accessed September 3, 2023. https://www.centerforfamilyprocess.com/video.html.

Gates, Henry Louis, Jr. *The Black Church: This Is Our Story, This Is Our Song.* New York: Penguin, 2021.

Gilligan, Carol. "In a Different Voice: Women's Conceptions of Self and of Morality." *Harvard Educational Review* 47, no. 4 (1977): 481–517. https://doi.org/10.17763/haer.47.4.g6167429416hg5l0.

Goodman, Marianne, David Carpenter, Cheuk Y. Tang, Kim E. Goldstein, Jennifer Avedon, Nicolas Fernandez, Kathryn A. Mascitelli, et al. "Dialectical Behavior Therapy Alters Emotion Regulation and Amygdala Activity in Patients with Borderline Personality Disorder." *Journal of Psychiatric Research* 57 (October 2014): 108–16. https://doi.org/10.1016/j.jpsychires.2014.06.020.

Gordon, Wayne, and John M. Perkins. *Making Neighborhoods Whole: A Handbook for Christian Community Development.* Downers Grove, IL: InterVarsity Press, 2013.

Green, John. *The Anthropocene Reviewed: Essays on a Human-Centered Planet.* New York: Dutton, 2021.

———. *The Fault in Our Stars.* New York: Penguin, 2012.

Guétin, Stéphane, Florence Portet, Marie-Christine Picot, C. Pommié, Mohsen Messaoudi, Leila Jemmi-Djabelkir, A. L. Olsen, M. M. Cano, Edith Lecourt, and Jacques Touchon. "Effect of Music Therapy on Anxiety and Depression in Patients with Alzheimer's Type Dementia: Randomised, Controlled Study." *Dementia and Geriatric Cognitive Disorders* 28, no. 1 (2009): 36–46. https://doi.org/10.1159/000229024.

Habermas, Jürgen. *The Theory of Communicative Action.* Vol. 2, *Lifeworld and System: A Critique of Functionalist Reason.* Translated by Thomas McCarthy. Boston: Beacon Press, 1987.

Haight, Roger. "Comparative Ecclesiology." In *The Routledge Companion to the Christian Church*, edited by Gerard Mannion and Lewis S. Mudge, 387–401. New York: Routledge, 2008.

Harrison-Jones, Winterbourne. *Final Formative Power Grant Report.* Witherspoon Presbyterian Church, 2021.

Hauerwas, Stanley. *Approaching the End: Eschatological Reflections on Church, Politics, and Life.* Grand Rapids, MI: Eerdmans, 2013.

Heath, Chip, and Dan Heath. *The Power of Moments: Why Certain Experiences Have Extraordinary Impact.* New York: Simon & Schuster, 2017.

Helson, Ravenna, and Christopher J. Soto. "Up and Down in Middle Age: Monotonic and Nonmonotonic Changes in Roles, Status, and Personality." *Journal of Personality and Social Psychology* 89, no. 2 (2005): 194–204. https://doi.org/10.1037/0022-3514.89.2.194.

Hewitt Suchocki, Marjorie. *In God's Presence: Theological Reflections on Prayer.* St. Louis: Chalice Press, 1996.

———. *21 Psalms for the 21st Century: Process Meditations.* Anoka, MN: Process Century Press, 2023.

Heyns, L. M., and H. J. C. Pieterse. *A Primer in Practical Theology*. Pretoria: Gnosis, 1990.

Hightower, James E., Jr. *Caring for People from Birth to Death*. New York: Routledge, 1999.

Hoffman, Jessica, and Sandra Russ. "Pretend Play, Creativity, and Emotion Regulation in Children." *Psychology of Aesthetics, Creativity, and the Arts* 6, no. 2 (2012): 175–84. https://doi.org/10.1037/a0026299.

Holmes, Jeremy. *John Bowlby and Attachment Theory*. 2nd ed. East Sussex: Routledge, 2014.

"Indiana Avenue." Discover Indiana. Accessed September 1, 2023. https://publichistory.iupui.edu/items/show/242.

Internet Encyclopedia of Philosophy. "Dietrich Bonhoeffer (1906–1945)." Accessed October 24, 2023. https://iep.utm.edu/dietrich-bonhoeffer.

Jana, Tiffany, and Michael Baran. *Subtle Acts of Exclusion: How to Understand, Identify, and Stop Microaggressions*. 2nd ed. Oakland: Berrett-Koehler, 2023.

Jill-Levine, Amy. *The Difficult Words of Jesus*. Nashville: Abingdon Press, 2021.

Jung, C. G. *Psychology of the Unconscious*. Mineola, NY: Dover, 1912.

Kärkkäinen, Veli-Matti. *An Introduction to Ecclesiology: Historical, Global, and Interreligious Perspectives*. Downers Grove, IL: IVP Academic, 2021.

Kegan, Robert. *In Over Our Heads: The Mental Demands of Modern Life*. Cambridge, MA: Harvard University Press, 1994.

Kelcourse, Felicity. *Human Development and Faith: Life-Cycle Stages of Body, Mind, and Soul*. 2nd ed. St. Louis: Chalice Press, 2015.

Kendi, Ibram X. *Stamped from the Beginning*. New York: Bold Type Books, 2016.

Kiros, Teodros, ed. *Explorations in African Political Thought: Identity, Community, Ethics*. New York: Routledge, 2013.

Lawndale Christian Community Church. "About Our Lead Pastor." Accessed September 23, 2023. https://lawndalechurch.org/bio.html.

Lemmons, Kasi, dir. *Harriet*. Focus Features, 2019. DVD.

Levinas, Emmanuel. *Ethics and Infinity: Conversations with Philippe Nemo*. Translated by Richard A. Cohen. Pittsburgh: Duquesne University Press, 1985.

———. *Totality and Infinity: An Essay on Exteriority*. Translated by Alphonso Lingis. Pittsburgh: Duquesne University Press, 1969.

Lewis, Stephen, Matthew Wesley Williams, and Dori Grinenko Baker. *Another Way: Living and Leading Change on Purpose*. St. Louis: Chalice Press, 2020.

Liddicott, Sam. "Natural Selection: Why Music from Our Childhood Stays with Us." Music Musings and Such. Accessed September 2, 2023. https://www.musicmusingsandsuch.com/musicmusingsandsuch/2017/10/15/feature-natural-selection-why-music-from-our-childhoodstay-with-us#.

Liebert, Elizabeth. *Changing Life Patterns: Adult Development in Spiritual Direction.* St. Louis: Chalice Press, 2006.
Loder, James E. *The Logic of the Spirit: Human Development in Theological Perspective.* San Francisco: Jossey-Bass, 1998.
Love, Velma E. *Divining the Self: A Study in Yoruba Myth and Human Consciousness.* University Park: Pennsylvania State University Press, 2012.
Lowery, Stephanie A. *Identity and Ecclesiology: Their Relationship among Select African Theologians.* Eugene: Pickwick Publications, 2017.
Madison, James H. *The Ku Klux Klan in the Heartland.* Bloomington: Indiana University Press, 2020.
Main Street United Methodist Church. "Grow Deeper." Accessed September 23, 2023. https://www.mainstreetumcboonville.com/serve.
Mannion, Gerard, ed. *Comparative Ecclesiology: Critical Investigations.* London: T&T Clark, 2008.
Marsh, Charles. *Strange Glory: A Life of Dietrich Bonhoeffer.* New York: Vintage, 2014.
McClure, John S. *Other-Wise Preaching: A Postmodern Ethic for Homiletics.* St. Louis: Chalice Press, 2001.
———. *The Roundtable Pulpit: Where Leadership and Preaching Meet.* Nashville: Abingdon Press, 1995.
McPhee, John. *A Sense of Where You Are: Bill Bradley at Princeton.* New York: Farrar, Straus & Giroux, 1999.
Minor, Cheryl V. *Godly Play in Middle and Late Childhood.* New York: Church Publishing, 2022.
Mitchem, Stephanie Y. *Introducing Womanist Theology.* Maryknoll, NY: Orbis, 2002.
Montessori, Maria. *The Montessori Method.* New York: Frederick A. Stokes, 1912.
Moore, Clarence C., and Jeff Krajewski. *Shades of Hope* (podcast). https://podcasts.apple.com/us/podcast/shades-of-hope/id1566911716.
———. "Worship as One." New Era Church, April 30, 2023. Video, 38:12. https://www.youtube.com/watch?v=-4LVg_MvC0M&t=331s.
Moore, Lecrae. Foreword to *The Color of Compromise: The Truth about the American Church's Complicity in Racism*, by Jemar Tisby, 17. Grand Rapids, MI: Zondervan, 2019.
Nelson, Shasta. *Frientimacy: How to Deepen Friendships for Lifelong Health and Happiness.* Berkeley: Seal Press, 2016.
North Carolina State University. "Teaching and Learning according to Paulo Freire." Accessed September 5, 2023. https://faculty.chass.ncsu.edu/slatta/hi216/documents/Freire_ed.htm.
Nunnelley, William. "Bonhoeffer Saw American Racism during Year of Study at Union Seminary." Samford University, January 9, 2017. Accessed

September 3, 2023. https://www.samford.edu/news/2017/01/Bonhoeffer-Saw-American-Racism-During-Year-of-Study-at-Union-Seminary.

Patton, John. *Pastoral Care in Context: An Introduction to Pastoral Care.* Louisville: Westminster John Knox Press, 1993.

Payne, Essie Kathryn Scott. *Mama and the Hills of Home: My Spiritual Pillars.* Azure Venture Publishing, 2002.

Poling, James. *Foundations for a Practical Theology of Ministry.* Nashville: Abingdon Press, 1985.

Ramsay, Nancy. *Pastoral Care and Counseling: Redefining Paradigms.* Nashville: Abingdon Press, 2004.

Rendle, Gil. "Leadership Means 'Pushing People to Purpose.'" *Faith & Leadership*, May 31, 2016. Accessed October 24, 2023. https://faithandleadership.com/gil-rendle-leadership-means-pushing-people-purpose.

Rieff, Philip. *The Triumph of the Therapeutic: Uses of Faith after Freud.* Chicago: University of Chicago Press, 1966.

Rogers, Fred. *The World According to Mister Rogers: Important Things to Remember.* New York: Hachette, 2019.

Root, Andrew. *The Congregation in a Secular Age: Keeping Sacred Time against the Speed of Modern Life.* Grand Rapids, MI: Baker Academic, 2021.

———. *Faith Formation in a Secular Age: Responding to the Church's Obsession with Youthfulness.* Grand Rapids, MI: Baker Academic, 2017.

Russell, Helene, and K. Brynolf Lyon. "Positioning Practical Theology: Contextuality, Diversity and Otherness." *Encounter* 72, no. 1 (Spring 2011): 11–30. https://www.proquest.com/scholarly-journals/positioning-practical-theology-contextuality/docview/874991149/se-2.

Russell, Letty M. *Just Hospitality: God's Welcome in a World of Difference.* Louisville: Westminster John Knox Press, 2009.

Sawicki, Marianne. *Seeing the Lord.* Minneapolis: Fortress Press, 1994.

Sawyer, Keith. "The Cognitive Neuroscience of Creativity: A Critical Review." *Creativity Research Journal* 23, no. 2 (2011): 137–54. https://doi.org/10.1080/10400419.2011.571191.

Scott, A. O. "Harriet Review: Becoming Moses." *New York Times*, October 31, 2019. Accessed December 7, 2023. https://www.nytimes.com/2019/10/31/movies/harriet-review.html.

Scott, Bernard Brandon. *Hear Then the Parable: A Commentary on the Parables of Jesus.* Minneapolis: Fortress Press, 1989.

Scott, Kim. *Radical Candor: Be a Kick-Ass Boss without Losing Your Humanity.* New York: St. Martin's, 2017.

Segovia, Fernando F., and Mary Ann Tolbert, eds. *Reading from this Place.* Vol. 1, *Social Location and Biblical Interpretation in the United States.* Minneapolis: Augsburg Fortress, 1995.

Shapiro, Tim. *How Your Congregation Learns: The Learning Journey from Challenge to Achievement.* Lanham, MD: Rowman & Littlefield, 2017.

Shapiro, Tim, and Kara Faris. *Divergent Church: The Bright Promise of Alternative Faith Communities.* Nashville: Abingdon Press, 2017.

Sheppard, Phillis Isabella. "The Current Shape of Womanist Practical Theology." In *Self, Culture, and Others in Womanist Practical Theology,* 41–60. New York: Palgrave Macmillan, 2011.

Singha, Shagun, Melissa Warr, Punya Mishra, Danah Henriksen, and the Deep-Play Research Group. "Playing with Creativity across the Lifespan: A Conversation with Dr. Sandra Russ." *TechTrends* 64, no. 4 (May 2020): 550–54. https://doi.org/10.1007/s11528-020-00514-3.

Slade, Peter. *Open Friendship in a Closed Society: Mission Mississippi and a Theology of Friendship.* New York: Oxford University Press, 2009.

Smith, James K. A. *You Are What You Love.* Grand Rapids, MI: Brazos Press, 2016.

Springsteen, Bruce. "Tunnel of Love." Recorded 1987. Track 7 on *Tunnel of Love.* Columbia Records, cassette tape.

Steele, Les L. *On the Way: A Practical Theology of Christian Formation.* Eugene: Wipf and Stock, 1998.

Stuckey, Heather L., and Jeremy Nobel. "The Connection between Art, Healing, and Public Health: A Review of Current Literature." *American Journal of Public Health* 100, no. 2 (2009): 254–63. https://doi.org/10.2105/ajph.2008.156497.

"Survey: What Is Church For?" *The Point,* December 15, 2017. Accessed September 2, 2023. https://thepointmag.com/survey/what-is-church-for-pastors.

Thompson, Deanna A. *Crossing the Divide: Luther, Feminism, and the Cross.* Minneapolis: Fortress Press, 2004.

Thurman, Howard. *The Inward Journey.* Richmond, IN: Friends United Press, 1961.

Tillich, Paul. *The Courage to Be.* New Haven, CT: Yale University Press, 1959.

———. *Dynamics of Faith.* New York: HarperCollins, 1957.

Tisby, Jemar. *The Color of Compromise: The Truth about the American Church's Complicity in Racism.* Grand Rapids, MI: Zondervan, 2019.

Townes, Emilie M. "To Be Called Beloved: Womanist Ontology in Postmodern Refraction." In *Womanist Theological Ethics: A Reader,* edited by Katie Geneva Cannon, Emilie M. Townes, and Angela D. Sims, 198–99. Louisville: Westminster John Knox Press, 2011.

University of Notre Dame. "The Most Segregated Hour." Accessed September 23, 2023. https://sites.nd.edu/jamesbaldwin/2021/03/25/the-most-segregated-hour.

Vatican Council II. "Lumen Gentium: Dogmatic Constitution on the Church." 1964.

Viney, Donald Wayne, and George W. Shields. *The Mind of Charles Hartshorne: A Critical Examination.* Anoka, MN: Process Century Press, 2020.

Walker, Alice. *The Alice Walker Collection: Non-Fiction.* London: Weidenfeld & Nicolson, 2013.

———. *In Search of Our Mothers' Gardens: Womanist Prose.* New York: Houghton Mifflin Harcourt, 1983.

Wallis, Jim. *America's Original Sin: Racism, White Privilege, and the Bridge to a New America.* Grand Rapids, MI: Brazos Press, 2016.

Watkins Ali, Carroll A. *Survival & Liberation: Pastoral Theology in African American Context.* St. Louis: Chalice Press, 1999.

Watson, Natalie K. *Introducing Feminist Ecclesiology.* Eugene: Wipf and Stock, 1996.

Williams, Reggie L. *Bonhoeffer's Black Jesus: Harlem Renaissance Theology and an Ethic of Resistance.* Waco, TX: Baylor University Press, 2014.

Williamson, Marianne. *Illuminata: Thoughts, Prayers, Rites of Passage.* New York: Random House, 1994.

Winnicott, Donald W. *The Maturational Processes and the Facilitating Environment: Studies in the Theory of Emotional Development.* New York: Routledge, 1990.

Index

abortion, 143–44, 148
Abyssinian Baptist Church, 60–61
Actors Ink, 133–34, 137
adolescence, search for identity, 129
adult education, 143
adventurous congregations, 64
African Americans, 27–28; mass migration acknowledged by, 127; women theologians, 25. *See also* Black Church
African Methodist Episcopal tradition, 89
anecdotes and stories, 57–58, 122, 132–33; Adam (mathematician), 64; on being woman, 63; cat named Integration, 87–88; Moore, C., "Your Father," 97–98; on shadow side of church, 61–62; valedictorian rejection, 81–82
antiracism, 27–28
anti-Semitism, 60
Apostle Paul, 33–34, 38, 67
arts: as life arena, 4, 150; religious teachings through, 130, 131
Asante Art Institute, 134

Ash Wednesday, pastor on being seen during, 37–38
atonement theology, 106
attachment (secure attachment), 121, 155, 163; creativity and secure, 129; eye-to-eye connections and, 137; Hope Church choosing, 144; intergenerational relationships and, 137; as mutual trust, 86; testing security of, 137; theory, 69, 102, 108–9, 129
authority, 73–74, 96–98, 156

baptism, 52, 60–61
Beatitudes, 46
being seen, 37–38
beliefs: embodying, 31; identity, activity and, 20–23, *20–23*, 27–28, 55–56
belonging, 162–63; Berry on, 56; Cunningham on, 11–12; identity formation through, 21–22
benedictions, 1
Berry, Wendell, 9, 56

178 Index

Bible: conversation and, 40; *eleutheros* in, 120; study, 152. *See also* Scripture; *specific passages*
BIPOC assemblies, 11
Black church: Bonhoeffer experience, 60–61; identity formation and music in, 55; Moore, C., on fear and, 96; social justice movement led by, 82
Black Jesus, 61
Black liberation theology, 25
Black Lives Matter, 134–35, 137; mural, 131–32, 140n11
blended family, 5–6
Bonhoeffer, Dietrich, 48, 59–61, 65; execution of, 58; on friendship, 105–6
Bonhoeffer's Black Jesus (Williams), 60
Boon, Ratliff (senator), 115
Boonville, Indiana, 115–16
Boonville Beginning (mural), 115–16
Bowen, Murray, 71
Bowlby, John, 69, 108–9
Bradley, Bill, 48
brain neurobiology, 76
Buber, Martin, 7
buildings, congregations without, 65
burnout, ministry, 8, 13n3
Buttrick, David, 43

California African American Museum, 27
care ministries, 153
CARES Act, 89
caring, for ill, 151
case study: on creative congregations, 131–38; imagined, 141; reflections, 137–38. *See also* Hope Church; Witherspoon Presbyterian Church
cat, named Integration, 87–88
Center for Congregations, in Indiana, 9; curriculum development, 10; formative process, 10–13; membership identity and, 56; mission statement, 10; pastor call to office of, 56–57
charity, as life arena, 151
Chaves, Mark, 53
children, 104, 128
Christian Community Development Association, 94
Christianity, racism and, 87
Christian Reformed congregation, 17
Christian Theological Seminary, 9
Christian virtue, 5
Christmas Eve service, 6
Chronos time, 77
church: Black, 55, 60–61, 82, 96; within church, 63; shadow side of, 61–62; Steele on "churchiantiy" and, 62; survey on purposes of, 17–18. *See also* congregational life; Hope Church; Main Street United Methodist Church; Witherspoon Presbyterian Church
"co-conspirators," 56
cognitive development model, of Piaget, 73, 128
cognitive engagement, creativity and, 129
college student, sociology connection made by, 53–54
The Color of Compromise (Tisby), 87, 88, 90
commensality, 114
Common Ground Church: "front-door welcome" and, 98; New Era and, 97–98; pastor of, 83, 87; pilgrimages of, 91–93, 117; racism complicity concern, 87–88

Communion of Reformed
Evangelical Churches (CREC),
17–18
community: of congregational
leaders, 162; creativity and, 130;
transitions, 133; vision for faith
communities, 164
comparative ecclesiology, 19
competence, 73, 109, 137
congregational life: aims of, 2;
"church" and, 18; contextual
theology of, 17–23; conversations
taking place in, 42; formative
assets of, 48–49; theology of, 18;
ways personal growth is nurtured
by, 32
congregational practices
(activities): Bonhoeffer and,
60–61; connecting life arenas
with, 153–55; defining,
52–54; faith and friendship,
112–13; Formative Power
project framework and, *136*;
formative process and, 11; in
growth framework, 4–5; guide
for connecting, 152–53, *153*,
157–58; identifying specific,
153–55; life arenas and, 153,
153; mentoring life arena and,
143; movies as, 114–15; music
and identity in, 54–55; partial list
of, 152; pilgrimages as, 93–95;
sacred and secular, 105; shared,
12; testimony as, 96–98, 115; as
vehicles of transformation for
Witherspoon Presbyterian, 138;
Venn diagram of life arenas, trail
markers and, *156*; worship, 96–98
congregations, 17; without buildings,
65; day to day operations of, 1,
10; elements of worship in, 53;
gathering places of, 51; guide
to survey of members, 151;
interviews with members of, 152;
invitation to, 148–49; meaning
making of, 12; new, 56; purpose
of, 7–10, 142; racial reconciliation
between two, 83–84, 97–98;
reasons for creating creative,
130–32, 135; reimagining, 63–65;
sociological and theological
views of, 53; with two preachers,
52–53; vision for, 159; vision for
future of, 164. See also guide, for
congregations formative projects;
leaders, congregational; *specific
churches*; *specific congregations*
conjunctive faith, 75
connections: arts and creativity
importance for, 130; eye-to-eye,
137; intergenerational, 146;
online, 103
contextual ecclesiology, 19–23
contextual practical theology, 23–24;
areas, *24*; womanist theology
model of, 25–27
contextual theology, of
congregational life, 17–23
contradictions, God and, 58–59
conversation: on divisive topics, 70,
148; emotional regulation during
difficult, 90–91; with Formative
Power team on life arenas,
151; intergenerational meetups
sparking, 146; lifeworlds as
shaped by, 33–34; meaningful *vs.*
unclear, 34; News of the Week,
143–44, 145; podcast, 90; power
of religious, 89–90; protection
from empty or confusing, 35;
Scripture as unlimited, 39–41;
testing secure attachment through
difficult, 137; ultimate concerns

revealed through, 44; unlimited, 33–34, 39–41, 90, 147
Cooper-White, Pamela, 77
Corinthians: 3:17, 120; 13:12, 38
Covid-19, 101–2, 133–34, 162; deaths and, 136
creation care, life arena of earth and, 151
creative congregation, forming: reasons for, 130–32, 135; Witherspoon Presbyterian Church case study, 131–37, *136*
creativity: connection and community through, 130; emotional regulation and, 128–29; as essential for growth, 127–28; intergenerational dynamics and, 135; members awakening to, 135; psychologist definition of, 127–28; secure attachments and, 129; social change and, 131–32; theological reflection and, 131
CREC. *See* Communion of Reformed Evangelical Churches
Crossan, John Dominic, 114
Cunningham, David, 11–12

dance, 130
desires, life arenas and, 45
Deuteronomy, 30:19, 31
developmental psychology, 3, 24, 68, 72
difficult conversations: about gun violence, 146–47; self-regulation during, 90–91; testing secure attachment through, 137
disagreement, 108, 148
Doulos (slave), 88
doulos, slave/servant translations, 111
Dykstra, Craig, 7, 32, 62–63

Easter poem, 6
ecclesia, 19
ecclesiological circle, 20–23, *20–23*
ecclesiology: biblical images and, 19; coalescing of practical theology with, 27–28; comparative, 19; contextual, 19–23; definition, 20; fields of practical theology and, 18; first use of term, 28n2; practical, 27–28; term, 19
education, 4, 144, 150
Einstein, Albert, 128
EJI. *See* Equal Justice Initiative
Eleutherian College, in Indiana, 120–21
eleutheros (freedom), 120
Emancipation Proclamation, 97
emotional regulation (self-regulation), 69–71, 109; creativity and, 128–29; definition, 155; during difficult conversations, 90–91
emotions: emotional center, 117; emotional safety, 161; identity formation and, 128–29; sketching helping to process, 127
enslavement, identity through music connections during, 55
Ephesians: 1:21, 33–34; 4:15–16, 67
Equal Justice Initiative (EJI), 91
Erikson, Erik, 72, 128–29, 133
Ethics and Infinity (Levinas), 37
existential theology, 145
external disruptions, 161–62

Facebook, 34
faith: arts and transcendence link with, 130; dissonance inherent in, 59; Fowler on stages of, 75; friendships as building, 112–13; life arenas and, 31, 46; measuring, 122; Tillich on ultimate concern

of, 43; unlimited conversation
and, 39
family: as life arena, 4, 28,
150; personal experience of
blended, 5–6
family systems theory, 91
fellowship meals, 147, 153
female relationships, transformative
power of, 145
feminist theologian, 106
field trip, challenging, 146–47
finances, as life arena, 4, 150
Fisher, Albert, 60
Floyd, George, 161–62
formation, Christian, 2; formative
theory of God, 63–65
formation, congregational, shadow
side, 61–63
Formative Power
project: beginning, 141–46; case
study implementation of, 146–48;
creating team for, 142, 149;
curriculum, 74; framework, *136*;
future vision for, 164; impact,
121–22; impact quotes, 122–23;
interviews, 142; invitation, 148–
49, 163; key themes, 160–63;
as overdetermined, 113–14;
participant comments, 161, 162;
pastor and congregation formed
by, 135–37; Pimlott's team of,
103; principle underpinning,
142; on trail markers, 11, 68,
136; ultimate concerns shared by
participants, 45–46; Witherspoon
and, 135. *See also* guide; human
development
formative process, 10–13
Fowler, James, 75
framework: Formative Power
Program, *136*; human
development, 3–5

Friedman, Edwin Howard, 71
friendships: as atonement, 106;
educational events as catalysts
for, 116–17, 124; faith built by,
112–13; intergenerational, 107,
123–24, 147; Jesus need for,
110–13; as life arena, 102–4; pie-
making and, 105–8; "third thing"
requirement for, 107

Galatians: 3:27–29, 119; 5:22–23, 67
Galilee, 42–43, 46, 48
Generation to Generation
(Friedman), 71
Genesis, 35
Gilligan, Carol, 73–74
God: between-people existence of,
105; congregational purpose of,
142; contradictions and, 58–59;
formative theory of, 63–65;
growth in relationship with, 121;
as relational, 21; synchronicity
of, 119
Gordon, Wayne "Coach," 94
Gospel of Mark, 39–40, 42
Got Something to Say, 134
Green, John, 64, 143
growth. *See* human development
guide, for congregations formative
projects: step 1: create
Formative Power team, 149;
step 2: first gathering, 149;
step 3: introduce life arenas,
150, 150–51; step 4: facilitate
discussion with team, 151;
step 5: congregational query,
151–52; step 6: connect life arena
with congregational practices,
152–53, *153*; step 7: identify
specific congregational practices,
153–55; step 8: explore trail
markers with team, 155–56, *156*;

step 9: process for combining all elements, 157–58
guilt, 59, 72
gun violence, 146–47, 148

Habermas, Jürgen, 33–34, 90
Harriet, 114–15, 122
Harrison-Jones, Winterbourne LaPucell (Rev. Dr.), 138; Actors Ink and, 133–34; formation of, 135–37; as Witherspoon pastor, 132–33
Hart, Betty, 114
Hauerwas, Stanley, 20–21
Heath, Chip, 116–17
Heath, Dan, 116–17
Hebrews, 13:13, 63
historically Black colleges, 89–90
History of Race in American Film (class), 109–10, 114, 117
Hitler, Adolf, 58
hobbies, life arena of, 151
holding environment, 161
homophobia, 138
Hope Church (imagined case study): beginning Formative Power, 141–46; diverse reactions and growth, 147–48; fellowship meals, 147; Formative Power implementation, 146–48; life arenas and congregational practices stage, 143–44; News of the Day events, 146–47; News of the Week conversations, 143–44, 145; polarizing topics and, 148; refocusing phase, 148; surveys and, 152; team creation and interviews, 142; trail markers stage of formation, 144
HR. *See* human resources
human development (personal growth), 2, 132–33; arts link with theology and, 130; Christian virtue and, 5; congregational shadow and, 61–63; contemporary and pastoral reflections on, 76–77; creativity as essential for, 127–28; discipline of, 5; formative assets of congregational life and, 48–49; God's purpose for congregations as, 142; how congregations nurture, 32; ingredients, 113–14; liminal experiences contribution to, 91–93, 116, 161; markers of, 52; from meaningful conversations, 34; measuring, 122; as never ending, 40; nonlinear concepts of, 77; settings for, 51; social environment influence on, 76; stage-oriented view of, 76–77; three-part framework and elements of, 3–5; trail markers and, 11, 68, *136*; women's reality and, 63. *See also* formation, Christian; Formative Power project; trail markers, of personal growth
"Human Development in Relational and Culture Perspective" (Cooper-White), 77
human resources (HR), 32–33

identity: beliefs, activity and, 20–23, *20–23*, 27–28, 55–56; creativity and, 128–29; Ecclesiological Circle of, *20–23*; Erickson model of stages of, 133; membership names and, 56; music and, 54–55; religion of, 109
Imani Community Wellness Program, 134
Imani Wellness Project, 133–35, 138

Index

impact: quotes, 122–23; results *vs.*, 122
improvisation, 155
In a Different Voice (Gilligan), 73–74
incarnation, 112–13
Indiana Historical Society, 75
Indiana Public Library, 75
initiative, 72, 91, 155, 160
integration, 59, 109–10, 115; cat named after, 87–88; definition, 156; of good and bad, 74–75; racial reconciliation and, 86–89
interconnectedness, Ubuntu concept of, 26
intergenerational relationships: attachment and, 137; creativity and, 135; friendships and, 107, 123–24, 147; Imani Community Wellness Program and, 134; meetups, 146; in mentoring, 143
interviews, 142, 152
invitation, to Formative Power project, 148–49, 163
isolation: from Covid-19 measures, 101–2; of Jesus, 111
IUPUI School of Education, 134

James (Bible passage), 42
Jamie (HR director), 32–33
Jesus: ethic of, 114; friends needed by, 110–13
John: 4, 91; 15:15, 111
John A. Roebling Suspension Bridge, 96
"Journey in Search of Justice," 134
Jung, Carl, 61

Kairos time, 77
Kegan, Robert, 37, 64
Kevin (high school student), 36–37
King, Martin Luther, Jr., 27

Kitchen Class, 102, 109
Klein, Melanie, 74
Krajewski, Jeff (pastor of white church), 83; antiracism preaching of, 92–93; conversations with Moore, C., 89–90; friendship with Moore, 84–85; social justice metacognition of, 95; social justice sermon of, 88
Ku Klux Klan, 83–84, 160–61

Lawndale, Chicago, 94
Lawrence, Jacob, 127
leaders, congregational: Center for Congregations and, 10; community of, 162
Learn-Go-Do: eating together before classes, 113–14; History of Race in American Film class, 109–10, 114, 117; impact quotes at end of, 122–23; incarnation concept embodied by, 112–13; as initiative example, 160; isolation inspiring project of, 103–4; pie-making class, 105–8; prayer explored during, 119; "third thing" and, 107
Legacy Museum, 91, 92, 99n13
Lepers, 101–2
Levinas, Emmanuel, 37
Leviticus, 20:7–8, 68
LGBTQ+, 138
life arenas, 160; arts as, 4, 150; being seen and, 37–38; connecting congregational practices and, 152–53, *153*; connecting trail markers to, 156, *156*; defined, 3; different selves and, 36–37; discussing with team, 151; education and lifelong learning, 144; the everyday and, 47; faith and, 31, 46; family as, 4, 28, 150;

Formative Power framework
and, *136*; friendships, 102–4;
Galilee as symbol for, 42–43;
guide for introducing, 150,
150–51, *151*; lifeworlds and,
33–34; list of various, 35–36;
mentoring, 143; Monday reality
and, 32–33; practical ecclesiology
and, 28; putting trail markers
and congregational practices
with, *156*, 157–58; racism, 138;
social justice, 84–85, 138; toxic,
62–63; ultimate concerns and,
43–48; unlimited conversation
and, 39–42; Venn diagram of life
arenas, trail markers and, *156*. See
also specific topics
Life Group, 8
lifelong learning, 144
Life Together (Bonhoeffer), 105–6
lifeworlds, Habermas on, 33–34
liminal experiences, 91–93, 116, 161
Little Man Tate, 93
Louisville Presbyterian Theological
Seminary, 9

Mahler, Margaret, 74
Main Street United Methodist
Church: Covid-19 isolation
experienced by, 101–2;
Eleutherian College pilgrimage
of, 120–21; five trail markers
explored by, 108–10; formative
components, 113–14; History
of Race in American Film class,
109–10, 114, 117; Kitchen Class,
102, 109; Learn-Go-Do project
and, 103–4; location, 115–16;
National Underground Railroad
Museum visited by members of,
117–18; pie-making class, 105–8;
postlude, 123–24; Richwood
Plantation visited by, 118. See
also Learn-Go-Do
Mama and the Hills of Home
(Payne), 81
Mary (mother of James), 42
Mary Magdalene, 42
mass migration, African
American, 127
Matthew: 5:6, 64; 5:9, 2; 8, 53–54;
20, 88; use of "slave" in, 88
membership: aging, 76; identity
and, 56
mental health, as life arena, 151
mentoring, 143
metacognition, 94, 95
"The Migration Series"
(Lawrence), 127
mindfulness, 70
ministry burnout, 8, 13n3
Mitchem, Stephanie, 25
Monday, life arenas and, 32–33
Moore, Clarence (pastor of Black
church), 83, 88; conversations
with Krajewski, 89–90; friendship
with Krajewski, 84–85;
storytelling of, 96–98
Moore, Lecrae, 87
morality, postconventional, 73–74
Moses, speaking to Israel, 31
movies, as congregational practice,
114–15
mural, Black Lives Matter, 131–32,
140n11
music, 54–55, 130, 152
mutual affection, 86
mutual authority, 74

National Memorial for Peace and
Justice, 91, 92, 99n13
National Museum of African
American History and Culture,
27–28

National Underground Railroad Freedom Center, in Cincinnati, 41, 95, 96, 117–18, 125nn13–14, 160
near-death experience, 62
neighbor, life arena of being, 151
neurobiology, 76
neuropsychology, 54
New Deal, 115–16
New Era Church: Common Ground and, 97–98; merger forming, 83; pilgrimage to National Underground Railroad Center, 96, 117; Westminster Presbyterian and, 84–85
Newfield Museum, 122–23
News of the Day events, 146–47
News of the Week, 143–44, 145, 148
New Testament, *eleutheros* in, 120
Niebuhr, Reinhold, 43
"no weapons allowed" sticker, 43–44

object relations theory, 74
Ohio River, 118
operations, congregational day-to-day, 1, 10

parables: conversations started by, 40–41; wedding banquet, 114
parenting, as life arena, 151
"pastoral," 24
pastoral theology, 23
pastors, 56–57, 83, 87, 135–37; "being seen" shared by, 37–38; expository style and, 52–53; pastoral care, 23–24, *24*; racial reconciliation between two, 89–90; survey of priests and, 17. *See also specific pastors*
Payne, Essie, 81–82, 87–88
Perkins, John, 94

personal growth. *See* Formative Power; human development
physics, modern, 64
Piaget, Jean, 73, 128
pie-making, friendships and, 105–8
pilgrimages, congregational, 91–95, 160–61; challenging field trip case, 146–47; Eleutherian College and, 120–21
Pimlott, Julie (Rev.), 101–4, 122
podcast, Moore, C., and Krajewski, 90
postconventional morality, 73–74
Powell, Adam Clayton, Sr., (Rev), 60
The Power of Moments (Heath, C./ Heath, D.), 116–17
practical ecclesiology, 27–28
practical theology, 18; coalescing of ecclesiology with, 27–28; contextual, 23–27, *24*; definition, 24
prayer, learning project exploration of, 119
preachers, 17, 52–53; ministry burnout and, 8, 13n3
preaching, 152
priests, survey of pastors and, 17
Psalm 23, 57
psychology, creativity definitions and, 127–28
Pye, Amy Boucher, 119

racial justice, 161–62
racial reconciliation: Common Ground pilgrimages as, 91–93; conversation between two pastors as, 89–90; integration and, 86–89; liminal experiences and, 91–93; Payne story and, 81–82; pilgrimages and, 93–95; through social justice life arena, 84–85; between two congregations,

83–84, 97–98; worship and testimony for, 96–98
racism: antiracism sermon, 27–28; Black Lives Matter mural and, 131–32, 140n11; Christianity as driving force of, 87; complicity, 87–88; life arena of, 138; race relations of 2020, 134; white congregants learning about, 82, 84
reconciliation, 73, 75. *See also* racial reconciliation
Reconstruction era, 6
religious conversation, 89–90
religious teachings, through arts, 130, 131
Rendle, Gil, 41
Reuther, Rosemary Radford, 19
Richwood on the River (formerly Richwood Plantation), 118, 125n14
Rieff, Philip, 62
rites of passage, 153
road rage, 69–70
Roosevelt, Franklin D., 115–16
"Rule of Life" booklet, 57

sacraments and rites of passage, 153
sacred arts and music, 130
Salome, 42
sanctification, 68
Sawicki, Marianne, 112
Schaeffer Institute, 13n3
school board visit, 146, 148
Schore, Allan, 76
scrapbooking, 75
Scripture, 2; as conversation, 39–42; friendship theme in, 110–13; goal of, 41; isolation theme in, 101–2; in Life Group meetings, 8; unlimited conversation in, 39–40. *See also specific passages*

Second Vatican Council, 19
secure attachment. *See* attachment
Seeing the Lord (Sawicki), 112
self-destruction, 62–63
self-differentiation, 71–72, 93; definition, 155; disagreements cultivating, 148; friendships bringing, 108
self-regulation. *See* emotional regulation
Selma, 115
sense of self, 36–38
A Sense of Where You Are (Bradley), 48
sermons: antiracism, 92–93; expository style of, 52–53; loneliness helped by, 103; social justice, 88; of Steele (Rev), 62
7 Ways to Pray (Pye), 119
Shades of Hope (podcast), 90
shadow side, 61–63
shyness, 6
Sindlinger, Verne (Rev.), 6
sketching, emotional processing through, 127
slave pens, 117, 119, 125nn13–14
slavery, 99n13; *doulos* in John 20, 111; Mathew 20 and, 88; plantations, 118; river pathway away from, 96
Smith, James K. A., 45
social change, creativity and, 131–32
social injustice, life arena of, 138, 150
social justice, 4, 82, 88, 93
sociology, 53–54
soul craft, 106
Stages of Faith (Fowler), 75
Steele, William (Rev.), 62
Stevenson, Bryan, 91
"Swing Low, Sweet Chariot," 55
synchronicity, 119

Index   187

teaching, as life arena, 151
testimony, congregational practice of, 96–98, 115
theology: arts link with, 130; atonement, 106; of congregational life, 18; contextual practical, 23–24, *24*; existential, 145; reflection and creativity, 131; womanist, 25–27, 47, 121, 145
Thompson, Deanna (feminist theologian), 106
Thurman, Howard, 12–13, 135, 164
Tillich, Paul, 43, 95
Tisby, Jemar, 87, 88, 90
Tolbert, Mary Ann, 36
Tower of Babel, 35
trail markers, of personal growth, 11, 59, *136*; authority, 73–74, 96–98, 156; competence, 73, 109, 137; emotional regulation, 69–71, 90–91, 109, 128–29, 155; guide for connecting, 152–53, *153*, 157–58; guide for exploring with team, 155–56; Hope Church and, 144; initiative, 72, 155, 160; list of, 68; Main Street United Methodist Church exploration of, 108–10; physical growth measurement and, 67; putting congregational practices and life arenas with, *156*, 157–58; self-differentiation, 71–72, 93, 108, 148, 155; transcendence, 75–76, 91–93, 130, 155–56; value of identifying, 77; Venn diagram, *156*; Witherspoon case study and, 137. *See also* integration
transcendence, 75–76, 91–93, 130, 155–56
travel, 152; pilgrimages and, 91–92, 93–95, 120–21
Trinity, 21

The Triumph of the Therapeutic (Rieff), 62
Tubman, Harriet, 114–15
twelve-step groups, 45

Ubuntu, 26
ultimate concerns, life arenas and, 43–48
Underground Railroad, 110. *See also* National Underground Railroad Freedom Center, in Cincinnati
Union Theological Seminary, 60
United Methodist Church, 75. *See also* Main Street United Methodist Church
United Negro College, 89–90

Van Gogh, Vincent, 122–23
vision, for future, 164
vocation, as life arena, 4, 150

wedding banquet parable, 114
wellness: Imani Wellness Project, 133–35, 138; as life arena, 4, 150; whole-person, 9
Westminster Presbyterian Church, 81; greetings after services, 103; New Era and, 84–85; Payne and, 87–88
What Are People For (Berry), 9
Wilberforce University, 89
Williams, Reggie L., 60
Winnicott, Donald, 74
Witherspoon Presbyterian Church: Black Lives Matter mural near, 131–32, 140n11; case study, 131–37, *136*; case study reflections for, 137–38; developmental stage of, 132–33; Imani Wellness Project of, 133–35; origin story of, 132–33; pastor

formation, 135–37; vehicles of transformation for, 138
womanist theology, 25–27, 47, 121, 145
women of color, female relationships and, 145
worship, 12, 53, 96–98

"Your Father" (in story told by Moore, C.), 97–98
youth group, 36–37, 93–94

Zionsville, 94

About the Authors

Rev. Dr. Christina Jones Davis, ThD, LMFT, currently serves as assistant clinical professor of pastoral theology and marriage and family therapy at Christian Theological Seminary (CTS). Dr. Davis's research and teaching interests focus on spiritually integrated therapy approaches, substance abuse and addiction treatment, relational psychoanalytic theory, and self-state multiplicity among women of color. Accordingly, Professor Davis has taught courses such as Foundations of Pastoral Care and Counseling, Theological Perspectives on Pastoral and Spiritual Care, Social and Cultural Dimensions of Counseling, Psychodynamic Family Therapy, Womanist Pastoral Theology, and Introduction to Marriage and Family Therapy Theory.

Prior to joining the faculty of CTS in 2014, Dr. Davis accumulated a decade of experience in pastoral care and counseling. Her passion has long been to serve local churches through mental health advocacy, training, and resourcing. She is a licensed marriage and family therapist and an ordained minister in the Progressive National Baptist Church and holds a ThD in pastoral care and counseling from Emory University's Candler School of Theology, where she was bestowed with the W. E. B. DuBois Noomo Award for Academic Excellence, as well as an MDiv and BA from Emory. When not teaching or training counseling students, Dr. Davis maintains a private practice providing therapy to individuals, couples, and families. Dr. Davis also enjoys time biking, gardening, and traveling with her partner, Ryan, and her two children, Madison and Carter.

Rev. Tim Shapiro, DMin, is the president of the Center for Congregations in Indiana, which he began serving in 2003 after eighteen years in pastoral ministry. The Center's mission is to strengthen congregations by helping them find the best resources to address their challenges and opportunities. The Center has worked with over half of Indiana's congregations.

For fourteen years, Tim served Westminster Presbyterian Church in Xenia, Ohio. Prior to that, he was pastor of Bethlehem Presbyterian Church in Logansport, Indiana. He holds degrees from Purdue University and Louisville Presbyterian Theological Seminary and is certified in positive deviance and homiletic supervision.

Tim's interest in how congregations learn to do new things is represented in his book *How Your Congregation Learns*. After extensive work on the Center's Sacred Space initiative, he coauthored the book *Holy Places: Matching Sacred Space with Mission and Message*. Along with colleague Kara Faris, he authored *Divergent Church*, a volume of case studies identifying characteristics of new expressions of being a church. He has also authored several articles, including "Applying Positive Deviance" and "The Congregation of Theological Coherence." In addition to the formative power of congregations, his current interest is in the application of contemporary academic theological and sociological research for congregational leaders.

Rev. Shapiro is an avid photographer and enjoys riding the excellent bike trail between Xenia, Ohio, and Yellow Springs with his wife, Gretchen Gale, and their three sons.

www.ingramcontent.com/pod-product-compliance
Lightning Source LLC
Chambersburg PA
CBHW071419160426
43195CB00013B/1749